"Design and Live the Life You *Love* is an amazing book that will open your mind and heart. Jo Anna is an incredibly insightful guide who leads you to dig beneath the surface of your everyday challenges to connect with your Deep Wisdom, so you can enjoy the quality of relationships and life you seek. Her radical truth-telling, poetic inspiration and tools will definitely help you live your greatest life!"

—**Norma Nakai Burton**, Unity in Ashland Minister, Counselor and Founder of the Circle of Trust Center – www.circleoftrustcenter.com and Journey to Completion® – www.journeytocompletion.com

"Jo Anna has created a delightful "how-to" for navigating your inner world so you can change it for the better and fully live your life's purpose. Spiced with personal experiences and trial-and-errors of her inspiring life-journey, she gently shows the path to personal growth and engaging life from the 'Innate Power' available when cultivating clear perception. Each section is enriched with her poetry and suggested movements to activate the brain, adding depth to the transformational experience."

—**Dr. Jane Battenberg, M.A., D.C.H.,** author of *Eye Yoga: How You See is How You Think* www.changewithin.com

"Utilizing poetry, personal stories and practical tools, *Design and Live the Life* You *Love* offers you a whole brain approach to unleash your authentic power and reveal meaningful success in your life and livelihood."

—**Alissa Lukara**, author of *Riding Grace: A Triumph of the Soul* – www.ridinggrace.com and founder of Transformational Writers www.transformationalwriters.com

"You see what you think you see. In *Design and Live the Life* You *Love,* Jo Anna provides tools that you can use to bring clarity to what is. At any point in time you can find yourself at a 'crossroads moment'. Now is the time to pick this book up and take your next relevant step. The more tools you have in your tool bag the easier it is to build your 'temple'."

—**Rev. Rob Wheeler,** Spiritual Leader of Christ Unity Church of Medford, Oregon www.unitymedford.org

"In *Design and Live the Life* You *Love,* Jo Anna Shaw has written a wonderfully simple, yet thorough, guide to changing one's life step by step, painlessly. It is a lifelong companion, giving helpful clues and insights into every facet and aspect of accepting a new You, no matter what your age or stage of life."

"In the Introduction to the book, Jo Anna writes 'I call transformational events crossroads moments because provided we are willing to be fully honest with ourselves, they invite us to stop, pay attention, reflect, feel our feelings and connect with deep desires.' You are at a crossroad moment now as you hold this book. A new You is calling."

—**Judith Coates**, co-author of the *Jeshua, The Personal Christ* series, and channel for Jeshua/Jesus. www.oakbridge.org

Design
and Live
the Life
You Love

A Guide for
Living in
Your Power
and Fulfilling
Your Purpose

Jo Anna Shaw, MBA

Rider & Ridden Press

Design and Live the Life *You* Love

Copyright © 2016 by Jo Anna Shaw

Published by:
Rider & Ridden Press
P.O. Box 604
Phoenix, OR 97535
www.joannashaw.net

Library of Congress Control Number: 2015959463

Softcover ISBN: 978-0-9971099-0-0
Ebook ISBN: 978-0-9971099-1-7

Illustrations by: Honey Metcalf
Cover Design and Layout by: Deborah Perdue, Illumination Graphics

To Kate,
Much Love
and Many Blessings
on your journey
Lena

For

ST and Julianna Forgione

and

Jaci Shaw

1954—2002

Acknowledgments

*B*ringing this guidebook to fruition challenged me to live every aspect of it over many years. A number of people were central to its gestation and birth.

In the early 90's I met Paul Dennison, Ph.D. and Gail Dennison, founders of Educational Kinesiology (Edu-K) and Brain Gym®. Their learning-through-movement model helped me embrace my learning style, overcome my writing and other blocks to success and awakened in me a desire to assist others with similar challenges. Much of the information and many of the activities for balancing the brain come from hundreds of hours of study with them. As a result of their encouragement, I created and offered to the Edu-K community an earlier version of the *Map Your Authentic Desires* guidepost. I appreciate our long-time friendship and the work Paul and Gail do in the world.

In 2000, Julianna and ST Forgione introduced me to their belief-change and energy work, additional tools and facilitation techniques that enabled me to build on what I learned in Edu-K. Their influence can be felt throughout this guidebook. *The Path of Mastery* guidepost (I call chapters "guideposts" to fit the book's theme) and many of the coaching tips I share are an outgrowth of our work together. I have said many times I would not be where I am today without Julianna's and ST's guidance and friendship.

In 2008, I joined my first writers' group facilitated by my friend Alissa Lukara of Transformational Writers, with the intention of writing a self-help book. At the time, I didn't know who my audience was or where to begin. To unlock my creativity, Alissa encouraged me to write for myself suggesting that if the book was to be for others, it would grow out of writing it for my own joy and benefit. During a year of participating in her writers' group and writing from her prompts, I began a memoir, small pieces of which made this guide, and decided to play with writing poetry. As my manuscript was taking shape, our every week or so walk in Lithia Park inspired me to trust the rewriting process, especially when I was frustrated with my progress. Alissa taught me that investing the time was the greatest gift I could give myself and others.

In 2009, Alissa encouraged me to read some of my poems at the "Open Mic Without a Mic" poetry night held once a month at the Downtowne Coffee Shop in Talent, Oregon. Afterward, she introduced me to Liz Robinson who surprised me with her appreciation of my poetry and an invitation to join a poetry circle in which she participated. The first poem in this book "Everything is Illuminated" was prompted by an email from Liz inviting all of her poetry friends to write a poem ending in those words. Most of my poems have been through at least one of our Saturday afternoon edit and encouragement rounds. I appreciate the unique contribution each member of my poetry circle has made to my development as a poet and writer: Kathy Dunn, Ines Diez, Charlotte Abernathy, Sally Ehrman, Dan Kaufman, David Hoffman, Beth Beurkens, Linda Barnes, Marisa Peterson and Sara-Lynne Simpson. The "Show, don't tell" mantra I learned from Alissa, Liz and all my poetry friends has taught me how to present this material in a way that invites the reader—through a unique presentation of a self-help journey—into wholeness.

My initial manuscript had only three poems. Now a poem greets you before the introduction, opens each guidepost and closes the book. Even now I am amazed at how delays in writing this allowed a new poem, perfectly suited as a transition into each guidepost, to emerge. "Twin Falls" was inspired by a David Whyte poem, "Dun Aengus" at a time I didn't think I was going to have a poem to bring to my poetry circle. "Riding Lesson" came from feedback on a horse poem I wrote early on that "...was at least four poems in one." "When", "Begin", "Moving" and "Breathtaking Closeness" started as journaling to ease my way through some transformational events. I wrote "Footsteps of Giants", the only poem not influenced by my poetry circle friends, when I saw how the Law of Attraction was working during the time I was teaching for a national business training firm. ST Forgione would regularly encourage me to "Write about it" when I was struggling with personal issues. The more I used writing in this way, the better my writing became. "Write about boxes" was one of his prompts that led to the poem, "Boxes". The closing poem, "T h e G a p", came of a quiet moment reflecting on my next steps once the book was published.

The *Projection Dilemma, Antagonist, Me, Inc. CEO, Projection, Inc. CEO* aspects of this guide and the tools in *Your Communication Toolkit* came together as part of a project I did for People's Bank of Commerce in 2012 and 2013. I appreciate Jeri Reno, the bank's Executive Vice President, for collaborating with me to address needs she had identified in the bank and Genie Gilliam, one of the bank's vice presidents and manager, for introducing me to Jeri. I give thanks for Jeri's and Genie's read-through and feedback on an early version of this guide, which helped me frame this material for a broad audience. More than the project that moved the creation of this book forward, I am grateful for the friendships that evolved during its development.

In addition to those already mentioned, I appreciate all the feedback I received from others who read my original manuscript at a point when I was ready to let it go and move on: Jonah Blue,

John Contreras, Lorna Romano, Karen Shaw and Cathy Keys. They inspired me to jump into major rewrites, build on the treasure hunt metaphor and follow my heart in choosing to merge poetry, self-help and my own personal growth memoir.

A special thank you to Lorna Romano for her frank, methodical, detailed and accurate editing. I appreciate her patience with my use or lack of punctuation, her encouragement and willingness to practice the principles outlined in this guide. I love that we have become great friends in the process.

No longer am I amazed at the synchronicity of how this guidebook came together. I know that its evolution—tracking with my own evolution—unfolded in the way it did for a purpose. Writing it helped me heal in ways I didn't know I needed to or could.

Contents

Contents

Foreword

𝒯he greatest honor a student can give a teacher is to take what she has learned, expand on it, and make it her own. In our eyes, Jo Anna has done that—not only with this guidebook but by the integrity with which she walks her talk as a teacher.

Through more than three decades we have facilitated thousands of sessions and workshops all over the world, teaching Educational Kinesiology (Edu-K), an in-depth system of intentional movement that we developed to empower learners and draw out innate potential.

We all have limitless capability to blossom in our own way at any stage of life. Many challenges, such as illness or trauma, can delay or interrupt the accessing of inborn gifts. And yet we find that adults and children can move beyond these factors at any age when they have desire, a playful attitude, and movements that stimulate their ever-growing brain.

Medicine and neuroscience now document the connection between movement, brain development, and learning, sharing our perception that movement activates the brain, optimizes learning, and helps alleviate stress and performance anxiety.

In the field of education, our niche has been assisting teachers and parents in creating optimal learning processes. Jo Anna is one of our early students who adopted the broader scope of our work, applying it to life as well as academic skills. She embraced it for her own personal growth as well as for the emotional and physical issues that adults and children experience when life and learning are difficult. This book weaves the story of Jo Anna's own growth with some of the self-help techniques that have served her and many others.

Enjoy the poems, stories, and activities in this guidebook. Through their application, you can embody the principles presented. You might want to reference this guide periodically, especially when you're at what Jo Anna calls a *crossroads moment*. Any issues with your family, school, work, or world can be resolved when you address them from your innate knowing.

This book will also help you to expand your awareness by understanding how your perception is affected by the physical learning skills you developed in your early years. These include the ability to focus both eyes for reading; to have eyes, hands, and ears cooperate when writing; and to achieve balance and congruence of words, tone, breath, and facial expression.

In its structure, Jo Anna's guidebook is similar to an Edu-K brain-balancing session. It reflects the tenets of Edu-K, drawing out learning by inviting you on a treasure hunt to mine your inherent potential—what Jo Anna calls your *Innate Power*. It asks you to benchmark your journey and hold an intention, because having an intention and noticing your growth are key to motivation, memory retention, and the mastery of new skills.

Design and Live the Life You *Love* incorporates Brain Gym® activities along with other tools designed to stimulate your brain so you can enhance your perception, notice what is supporting your growth, and shift away from what is not. It's presented in what we call a whole-brain way—balancing more left-brain, intellectual concepts with more right-brain-stimulating material. Together, these elements form a foundation for bringing balance, heart, and meaning to your life.

—Paul E. Dennison, Ph.D. and Gail E. Dennison,
creators of Brain Gym®, Educational Kinesiology,
and the *Hearts at Play: Move, Learn, Bloom* book series

"What can anyone give you greater than now,
starting here, right in this room, when you turn around?"

– William Stafford

"In each life there comes at least one moment which
if recognized and seized,
transforms the course of that life forever."
—Ralph Blum

Preface

*A*s I was writing this preface, I returned a call to a friend and got news that my ex-husband, Jon, had died unexpectedly. As far as anyone knew, he had not been sick. Walking down the street at the end of a day of doing the work that he loved, he dropped to the sidewalk and never got back up. If he had a life review upon departing this world, he would have celebrated that he followed his heart and did what he loved to do.

Two months after I first met Jon, the bank I was working for downsized and I took the option to leave my twenty-year banking career. With his encouragement, I started a new career, one hundred and eighty degrees from banking, in a rewarding field assisting adults and children with life, learning and behavior challenges. Ten years later, his exit from our marriage invited me to take my own healing journey to another level—to understand the part I played in the transformation of our relationship and overcome my own learning and behavior issues, which operated outside of my conscious awareness.

How I reacted to people arriving and departing from my life as well as the pull and push of my life events was pretty typical until I bottomed out on the couch ready to say yes to this invitation. Before this moment, I had been allowing things outside of me to influence whether I was happy or sad, worried or elated, angry or grateful. In this moment, I reached out for help, accelerating the adventure of learning how to truly live life in my Power.

Before I could recognize and seize that moment, I had been exploring different spiritual and personal growth paths motivated by my desire to know who I am, why I am here and how I might live happily and abundantly in my life. My search had led me out of a corporate career and into an alternative healing business. I had broken free of abusive relationships and entered healthy ones, but not without overcoming painful moments, financial hardships and health challenges along the way.

My banking career had enabled me to acquire all the trappings of the "American Dream" while continually struggling with my self-esteem, both at home and at work. In the early 1980s, my inability to manage the stress of an abusive relationship, a multi-state move and a new job led to health issues and I prayed for help (something I hadn't done since graduating from a Catholic elementary school). A synchronous meeting inspired me to begin reading self-help books, revisit my relationship with God and reinvent my life. I developed a growing interest in spirituality and self-help programs. Yet, no matter how much I practiced the recommended positive mental attitude, mindfulness, yoga, prayer and meditation activities, my self-doubt, low self-worth and self-criticism persisted.

Following my exit from the banking industry, I went against my worrisome banker's dire predictions and invested as much time as I needed in resting, reading and reflecting on why I continued to struggle with my self-esteem and what I wanted to do with the rest of my life. On sabbatical, I became aware that I had been mostly living or rebelling against the dreams of others up to that point in my life and I dedicated myself to discovering what *I* truly wanted and mastering how to live it. Since then, I have weathered a number of economic and relationship storms while staying true to this aim.

Today, I am no longer a victim of life's circumstances. To the contrary, I embrace, appreciate and use them to become a more authentic human being. Publishing this book is yet another crossroad rather than a destination in itself. My life continues to offer ongoing opportunities to realize the answers to the questions that motivate me.

My initial intention for writing this guide was to share lessons learned and some self-help tools and processes I found most useful in my recovery, as well as the grace I enjoy by living my life with this focus. I thought it would help you, the reader, engage relationship and work difficulties in a more meaningful way, benefitting from my experience. Humbly, I soon realized that I was writing this as much for me as you.

I have held each line up to the questions, *Am I walking what I talk about here?* and *Is this true?* Many rewrites have resulted in editing out judgmental comments, repetitions and unnecessary justifications as well as reordering dyslexic words, sentences and paragraphs. I came to value sometimes painful self-honesty while surrendering my agenda for its quick completion. Who I was becoming as a result of overcoming my obstacles to writing this guide was a priority over the business of creating a resource for others.

Being in a personal growth field has given me many opportunities to experience a variety of different approaches to resolving inner and outer challenges. Over time, I have found that techniques and activities presented in self-help books, workshops and seminars are important for opening the mind, building awareness, stirring desires and learning how to realize them. Yet we have a way of letting events, people and habits distract us from fully incorporating new ways of thinking and being into our daily lives.

My aspiration is that you follow through so you realize *your* true desires, wake up from dreams adopted from others and live consciously—that you embrace your crossroads moments and use them for remembering your life purpose, learning how to live in your Power and enjoying your rich tapestry of thoughts, feelings, senses and life experiences.

May you *Design and Live the Life You Love*, playfully engage obstacles at work and home, navigate unexpected detours and fulfill your life's purpose. And may your journey be rewarding in ways you, too, might not yet imagine.

Jo Anna Shaw

Everything is Illuminated

In now

there is a gap
where yesterday
and tomorrow
don't exist,

where
longing for what was and
hoping for what might be
disappear.

Faded photographs
and unrealized dreams
give way to
open hands.

Wondering
Why? and *What if?*
are relinquished
and
everything
is illuminated.

Introduction

Write Your Intention

For example, To be..., To feel..., To know...

Benchmark the Beginning of Your Journey

Briefly describe your current situation.
Include how you are presently thinking and feeling about it.

As you read through this guide and do its suggested activities,
periodically return to this page and notice how you and your life
are different.

"Whatever you can do, or dream you can, begin it.
Boldness has genius, power and magic in it."
—Johann Wolfgang von Goethe

Crossroads Moments

I call transformational events crossroads moments because provided we are willing to be fully honest with ourselves, they invite us to stop, pay attention, reflect, feel our feelings and connect with deep desires. We get the most from these moments when we find ourselves questioning everything we have ever done, believed and wanted. During these times, we may experience strong emotions. This is valuable. When we uncork bottled up feelings, we make room for a wellspring of thoughts and emotions to flow. Every crossroads moment holds the potential of awakening greater self-awareness, clarity, compassion and appreciation when we look for this treasure within it.

You have picked up this guide because you are at a crossroads moment. You may be thinking about where you have been, where you are and where you are going. You may know what you want but are struggling to achieve it. You may have finished raising your children or had some other major life event and are uncertain about your future. You may be frustrated with workplace systems or people and feeling powerless. You might be asking yourself pivotal life questions such as

Who am I? What is my purpose? and *How do I want to live the rest of my life?* These crossroads moments ask you to consciously do a life review and course correction before the end of your life so, when it is your time, you can look back happily knowing you fulfilled your life's purpose.

This guide is a resource for uncovering the treasure found within crossroads moments as well as the answers you seek. Rather than worrying about what to do, forcing a solution or doing nothing at crossroads moments, this guide invites you to consciously *Design and Live the Life You Love* and facilitates your next steps. As you discover, create and live the life *you* love, your greatest reward for choosing this approach is awakening an Innate Power remembered only by experiencing your unique quest.

"...your greatest reward for choosing this approach is awakening an Innate Power remembered only by experiencing your unique quest."

When the bank gave me the option to move on, I wanted to go in a new direction but I didn't know what that looked like at the time. After I packed my desk contents, turned in my keys and returned home from the bank, my plan was to take a few days to process my feelings and think about what to do next. Those few days turned into six weeks, much of it spent sitting on a lakeshore beach staring at the water and mountains in the distance as well as meditating, reading, dancing, riding horses and going to personal growth workshops. In spite of renewing my energy and motivation to get back to work in this way, I had no interest in filling out a resume and interviewing for another corporate position. Instead, I studied Educational Kinesiology, registered as a counselor and launched my own coaching and training business. I didn't know at the time that going in this direction would awaken my writing and intuitive gifts and grow me into being a mind-body coach touching many lives.

Making a one-hundred-eighty-degree career move required new skills, abilities and ways of thinking. My risk-averse banker's mentality had to yield so I could develop my healing abilities as well as my entrepreneurial heart and skills. My Educational Kinesiology training made me conscious of learning challenges I didn't know I had and gave me tools for overcoming them. I confronted negative thoughts and beliefs about my ability to succeed and created positive ones. Walking this path was made easier when I began viewing my work and personal life as a treasure hunt—a daily adventure in overcoming obstacles, learning from experience, uncovering my gifts and discovering my unique potential. Along the way, I developed a deep knowing that *the greatest treasure is not what I achieve; it's who I am becoming.*

"...the greatest treasure is not what I achieve; it's who I am becoming."

How To Use This Guide

I am not advocating that you go the way I have in my career or accept my insights. Your crossroads moments may lead you to a deeper commitment to the path you are currently on and your own insights, which may be different from mine. We each have our own unique potential and path for realizing it. Crossroads moments give you opportunities to discover or recommit to living yours.

Some crossroads moments can be overwhelming. It is beneficial to assimilate a major change at work, in health or in relationship before jumping to the next job or relationship. Once you have assimilated a crossroads moment, this guide is designed to facilitate your reflection and decision-making process. It is structured as a treasure map, complete with an overview of what to expect on the journey, how to prepare, clues that help you find your way and tools for overcoming obstacles and seeming detours—secondary crossroads moments—you are met with along the way.

Keeping with the treasure hunt theme, chapters are called Guideposts. Each provides you with clues and activities that encourage you to stop and reflect or take action. I picked this metaphor because crossroads moments can be difficult and painful or they can be inspiring and transformational. It all depends on your perspective, which you will discover has been shaped by your upbringing and the beliefs you formed as a result of it. The treasure hunt metaphor also helps you see the gems in your circumstances so you don't primarily focus on your problems.

Entering each guidepost, you will find my poetry and a quote that has inspired me on my journey, inviting you to pause and open your heart to what is coming. Together with the treasure hunt metaphor, they add a whole-brain element to what sometimes can be a mostly mental exercise. Before exiting each guidepost, you will find activities that also help you refine and sustain a whole-brain way of being as you engage crossroads moments and read this guide. You may choose to use them or not. I encourage you to listen to your intuition and do only what feels comfortable and appropriate for you.

A Self-Empowered Journey

"This journey is about living from your Power and trusting yourself."

Yes! This journey is about living from your Power and trusting yourself. You are in charge here. Run from anyone who professes to have your answers or the way to accomplish your goals. What you will read here is *a* way, not *the* way. I share what I have experienced and learned on my journey as well as stories of others who also walk this path. Your role is to embrace what you like and tailor it to you. You may even improve on my approach. Drop me a note if you do; I would love to learn from you. You may also set aside what doesn't speak to you. I maintain this self-empowerment theme each step of the way so you remember how to live from your Power. The letter "P" in Power and the first letter of every word that has this same meaning is capitalized throughout this guide when I refer to your Innate Power—the source of your wisdom, inspiration and courage.

Self-empowerment lays the foundation for getting the best from this or any other self-help program. A self-directed

"A self-directed approach begins with setting your intention."

approach begins with setting your intention. I use the word intention in a similar context as Dr. Wayne Dyer who wrote in *The Power of Intention,* "Intention isn't something you do, it is something you connect to." Setting your intention allows for the possibility of *This or something better.* It is a way of stating what you want then detaching from the outcome and the pathway there, following your intuition as you go. Before you set your intention, you may want to read through this whole guide first. Honor your learning style and approach this guide in whatever way works best for you. You will find it follows a specific sequence, which may or may not be the order that you will pick when you use it.

Once you know your intention, write it on page 2. Benchmark the beginning of your journey by adding a note describing the thoughts, feelings and circumstances that have led you to pick up this guide, then read through the guide again, reviewing the clues and doing the activities as you go. Throughout this guide you are given ways to address detours or obstacles you run into on your path. Keeping a daily journal is a great way of tracking your progress. Periodically, return to your benchmark and notice how your situation and your response to it are different.

Overview

Success with this or any self-help program comes from self-aware-ness, clarity of intention, keeping an open mind and commitment. The first four guideposts enable you to lay this foundation. The remaining guideposts show you how to navigate resistance from others as well as your own resistance to moving forward. They also help you experience your treasure throughout the journey, rather than at the end of it.

Guidepost 1 shows you how to *Reconnect With Your Innate Power.* Here you embark on the transformational adventure of remembering Essential You as well as how you veiled your Innate Power, how you can unveil it and how to enjoy living from it, especially when crossroads moments bring up confusion, frustration or a sense of powerlessness. If you react to circumstances or people while you are in one or more of these frames of mind, you may find yourself repeating patterns that contribute to undesirable outcomes. In this guidepost you will find activities for reconnecting with your Power and sustaining that connection as you *Design and Live the Life You Love.*

Guidepost 1 also shows you how your history taught you to disconnect from your Power and how that learning influences your present-time thoughts, feelings and senses. As you read, you will see that no one escapes being conditioned in childhood. By way of example, as the oldest of five who were born within six years of each other, I learned to focus on the needs of my parents and siblings. To take the tension off strained dynamics in our household, I became a pleaser and an over-achiever, losing touch with my feelings and desires. The gift of healing this conditioning is my ability to empathize with others, which contributes to my mastery of facilitating individual and group processes. The negative aspect of this conditioning is the habit of doing for others when I really need to take a time out. The clues, processes and activities presented throughout this guide are ones I have used or continue to use to unlearn what no longer serves me and develop the skills for living a healthy, happy and meaningful life, regardless of circumstances.

Guidepost 2 introduces clues that help you *Develop Innocent Perception.* These clues help you see how easy it is to misperceive events and interactions and how to stay open to other possibilities, so you make decisions from your Power. You will be guided through *Four Stages of Self-Awareness* and meet your primary obstacle to clarity, motivation and the ability to apply tools that move you forward. You will find awareness-enhancing tips and activities that enable you to unwrap the gifts found within crossroads moments so you can take your next steps mindfully and from your Power.

Guidepost 3 highlights why it is important to *Consciously Use Your Imagination.* Here you will find clues that invite you to reflect on your role in your challenges with people or ability to create what you want in your life. Other clues connect you with beliefs that fuel your imagination as well as more creative and productive ways to focus your thoughts and words. Before leaving this guidepost, you will also find tools for switching on your brain so you can make the best use of your imagination.

Guidepost 4 encourages you to *Map Your Authentic Desires*—to create *your* personal treasure map. Since the first three guideposts invite you to question whether the desires and goals you have aspired to (up to this point in your life) are adopted or truly your own, this guidepost gives you the opportunity to discover or reaffirm what *you* stand for and what *you* truly desire. Here you can develop or revisit *your Mission, Core Values, Vision* and *Goals* in the context of *your Purpose*—what you become as you accomplish each part—and map how *you* intend to live what you desire, each step of the way.

Guidepost 5 reveals clues for walking *The Path of Courage* as you journey through the mountains, valleys and wide-open plains of fulfilling your authentic desires. This guidepost shows you how to follow your treasure map and interact effectively when others object to your choices or doubt your ability to succeed. It addresses your own resistance to moving forward and offers additional tools enabling you to manage your emotions and courageously make the most of crossroads moments as you go for your treasure.

Guidepost 6 is *Your Communication Toolkit.* It is through your thoughts, words, feelings and actions that you follow your map and harvest your treasure. Guidepost 6 introduces you to or reminds you of listening and assertive communication skills as well as the *General Characteristics of Four Main Communication Styles.* It also offers examples that demonstrate how to apply these skills. The information in this guidepost is a summary of key skills that enable you to alter your current circumstances or gain support for going your own way.

Guidepost 7 guides you along ***The Path of Mastery,*** the fourth stage of self-awareness. It shows you how to notice areas where you can function more from your Power. There may come a time when repetitive challenges and situations seem to be the norm or where your outcomes consistently fall short of what you desire. In Guidepost 7, you learn how to read the clues within these types of crossroads moments and are provided with activities that empower you to eventually shift the cause of the effects you are experiencing.

Guidepost 8 invites you to ***Journey in Appreciation*** and enjoy its magnetic Power. Genuine appreciation is the key that unlocks the treasure chest of answers and solutions you seek, because it seeds clear perception. Activities in this guidepost enhance your ability to self-reflect, self-correct and self-motivate, so you engage crossroads moments from your Best Self. In Guidepost 8, you learn how to see the value, significance and magnitude of all your life experiences and complete your journey through this guide, while humbly knowing it is just another beginning.

Together, these guideposts are your map of how to *Design and Live the Life* You *Love* while *Living in Your Power and Fulfilling Your Purpose.* The most beneficial resolution of your crossroads moments comes about one day at a time, as you follow your treasure map.

This guide facilitates your footwork while synthesizing key elements from the many books I have read, therapy sessions I have experienced and insights I have gained through applying what I share here. And yet, this guide is not a substitute for outside support. As you read, if you become aware of a need for assistance, this guide will have you well prepared to know where you need guidance. There are many qualified experts who can support your journey. This guide empowers you to know what you need, trust the choices you make and direct your journey. It saves you time and money by offering you a self-empowered approach to what you would experience in the initial term of many individual coaching programs.

Why Refer to this Guide Regularly?

Life is continually presenting you with crossroads moments. Each one can be a benchmark measuring your progress. As you reflect on your crossroads moment(s), ask yourself, *Who is this person or event inviting me to become?*, *How am I giving my Power away?* or *What desire is this person or event inviting me to connect with?* If the answers to one or more of these questions are unclear, read through or revisit this guide. As you do, notice whether you are metaphorically missing diamonds that are buried in your own back yard or whether you are truly being guided to go in new directions. This is not a book to be read once and placed on a shelf. It is a workbook.

Each time you pick it up you may gain new insights or find an activity that advances you on your path.

When you live from your Power, you have access to the full spectrum of your own unique mental, emotional and physical abilities. You can know what you want and choose with ease because you can be logical and analytical as well as creative and intuitive. You can be self-aware as well as in tune with what is happening around you. You may favor some abilities over others, but will not exhibit dominance in one while inhibiting the others. In the field of Educational Kinesiology, which means learning through movement, this is called a whole-brain way of being. Many physical and creative activities balance your logical, linear, sequential, detail-oriented and expressive left-brain functions with your rhythmic, pattern-sensing, feeling, spacial, big-picture-oriented and receptive right-brain functions. The activities I mention in this guide are intended to bring about this balance. When your brain is balanced, your body lets you think, feel and act from your Power.

I didn't realize how out of balance I was until I was shaken up by many crossroads moments. Eventually, I decided I wanted to find another way. Each time I said *Yes* to walking the personal growth path through crossroads moments, I became happier, healthier and more fulfilled, no matter how they resolved. Still, I continue to ask *Is there more?* Following this thread of desire, I have found my speaking, writing and poetry voice, a deep well of compassion for myself and others, more consistent periods of inner peace, happiness and fulfillment, and a self-appreciation that sources a great desire to extend Love.

This guide invites you to follow your thread of desire as you go for your treasure and notice who you become as you do. You, too, may find the possibilities are limitless.

Guidepost 1:
Reconnect With Your Innate Power

Twin Falls

Well into a week of heavy rain,
drive thirty miles east of Seattle to North Bend.
Follow the exit signs to Twin Falls trailhead. Don full rain gear
and enjoy being a lone hiker along the swollen stream
through cathedral Ponderosas and White Pines.
Walk the snaking trail
about a mile to the pine-steel foot-bridge
suspended between upper and lower waterfalls.
Find center and face the dark purple pond
held by mammoth black stone walls
rounded by ancient flows spilling from above.
Marvel at the unknown depth that stills the raging water
before it crests the turtle-head point and disappears,
shattering on boulders three hundred feet below.
Stand timelessly.
Smell moss-wet air.
Sense roaring water vibrate inside your bones.
Feel mist washing away mind-chatter.
When you make your way back,
hike the narrow path left from the main trail
to the wooden lookout midway of the lower falls.
View water's fullest cascading surrender. You can
almost touch the crashing sheets of power.
Notice how small you are
in the presence of your mortality,
how insignificant the spills and crashes of your life.
Face the intensity of Mother Nature pouring her heart out.
Scream from your belly and notice
no matter how hard you try
you cannot drown the resonance

of the pounding water-wall.
Sit for a moment
and let its generous yielding
awaken in you
remembrance
of your Essential Power.
Exit the old growth forest alert.
Nature spirits will be celebrating
that you momentarily stepped away
from your stormy life,
visited their world,
let earth mother
quench your thirst.
Know
in every heightened cell
the secret pact
you make
here.

"Between stimulus and response there is a space. In that space is our power to choose our response. In our response lies our growth and our freedom."
—Viktor Frankl

The Gift of Crossroads Moments

*R*emember how you felt when you left home to live on your own for the first time? Excited; you could find or follow your passion and you didn't have to listen to mom or dad telling you what to do anymore. Remember your first "real" job? Free; you could make your own decisions, share your ideas, do what you wanted and finally have your own money to spend. Along with the send-off you received from your family, you may or may not be aware that the backpack you hoisted over your shoulder as you left home was filled with more than your clothes, technologies and a peanut butter and jelly sandwich. It was also filled with the "rules" you formed for surviving in your family system.

I put quotes around the word "rules" because they can include values, beliefs, responsibilities and commandments your parents, relatives, ministers, teachers and friends enforced or ones you formed in your imagination in response to the messages you received. These "rules" operate at a level below your conscious awareness driving your present-time thoughts, feelings and actions. It is like your hard-drive has been infected with a virus that causes startling pop-ups when least expected. When you react impulsively at major or minor crossroads moments, you have unpacked the "rules" and are using the same survival scripts you used back then. When your actions backfire and cause all sorts of undesired outcomes, they are probably driven by these "rules."

When I understood the information I share in this guidepost, I realized that negative unconscious programming was contributing to my health, work and relationship challenges. In the process of revoking these "rules," I also realized that my caregivers did the best they could at the time and that uncovering the treasure within my challenges was a mature response to them. The gift I found within crossroads moments was the opportunity to reclaim my Power so my choices and interactions would originate from It.

"The gift I found within crossroads moments was the opportunity to reclaim my Power so my choices and interactions would originate from It."

This guidepost reminds you of the qualities and wisdom you express when you are living in your Power, how to reconnect with them and how to sustain your connection. Subsequent guideposts show you how to unlearn what you have probably been practicing for a very long time and offer suggestions for re-educating your deeper mind, so your future actions are sourced increasingly from your Power. This guidepost provides you with your first set of clues. The first clue invites you to reframe your understanding of Power and your relationship to it, laying an essential foundation for uncovering the gems within your crossroads moments.

Clue #1: Power is a Neutral Force

As a child, when I fell off a horse my father would pick me up and put me back in the saddle while telling me, "If you don't get back on now, you never will." His Marine Corps Major "encouragement" gave me the strength to pick myself up and move on after his death, as well as after subsequent job and relationship losses. For most of my life before my 2001 crossroads moments, I lived out his "rules" by willing my way through challenges. As I did, I sacrificed my health, my deeper desires and treasured relationships.

The attack on the World Trade Center was one of many, back-to-back events that altogether brought me to my knees. Within the year, Jon and I had moved and married, my mom and one of my sisters had died within months of each other and his folks made their passing. Our relationship crumbling the week the towers came down was the hundredth chip on the carvers stone. I cracked. Powerless to make even the simplest of decisions, I reached out for help. I appreciate those who enabled me to find the will, courage and strength to pick myself up and go on in a more conscious and gentle way than I had before. With their help, I discovered a much deeper resilience and the strength to remember how Power had been misused on me early in my life. Like eating an artichoke, the tough petals gradually gave way to a tender, delicious center— *"I came to understand that my newfound vulnerability, which I had previously judged as weak, was a fundamental expression of that Power."* where I experienced my Innate Power. I came to understand that my newfound vulnerability, which I had previously judged as weak, was a fundamental expression of that Power.

During this time, I took up a nonviolent martial art called Aikido, a Japanese word that generally means the way of harmony with nature or the universe. I was attracted to Aikido while taking a workshop from an aikidoist who was using its activities to show us how to communicate more effectively with children and young adults. I found such value in this movement-based training metaphor, I was inspired to add Aikido activities to my workshop and self-development toolkits. As an unexpected benefit of practicing Aikido, I also refined my understanding of and relationship with my Power.

In Aikido, the belief that Power is either good or bad is dispelled. Power is a neutral force that can be used to *"Power is a neutral force that can be used to protect as well as harm, to heal as well as injure."* protect as well as harm, to heal as well as injure. Morihei Ueshiba (O'Sensei), the founder of Aikido said, "As soon as you concern yourself with the 'good' and 'bad' of your fellows, you create an opening in your heart for maliciousness to enter." Judging anything as good or bad limits our Power to think wisely and move accurately. These value judgments fuel emotion and reactive behavior. When I speak of our Innate Power, I am referring to Power as a neutral force.

If Power is neutral, then how it is expressed is determined by each individual who is free to apply it anywhere along a continuum encompassing *Misuse* at one extreme and *Best Use* at the other.

Misuse   Innate Power   Best Use

When Power is misused on us at a young age, we become conditioned to think that forcing solutions with a big voice or a strong arm or manipulating by withholding love and using a silent treatment is what Power is all about. We survive by forming our own misuses of Power like complying, fighting, running away or being resentfully quiet. The effects of experiencing early misuse of Power can be felt later in life. We may not speak up in groups or question people in authority. We may try to control people or situations. We may be quick in voicing our opinions. Or, we might avoid activities where we feel our Power, like public speaking or acting on our beliefs.

In my family and church community, Power was misused so I unconsciously formed a fear of It. I learned to be compliant, speak only when spoken to, step lightly so as not to be heard, doubt myself and struggle with decisions. Afraid to be direct, I would justify what I was going to say by going on and on about seemingly unrelated issues before making a point or asking for what I wanted.

One day, my coach brought my communication style to my attention when he said that he pictured me "...out in a field filled with a lot of bushes and beating around every one of them." His playful attitude in our work *"...a nonjudgmental, playful attitude is a best use of my Power."* together made it safe for me to upgrade the behaviors I had developed in reaction to past misuses of Power and modeled for me the lesson that a nonjudgmental, playful attitude is a best use of my Power.

Whether we become like those who misused Power on us or the extreme opposite of them, our Innate Power has been clouded by the belief that either we don't have any Power, or that the only way to get Power is by passively or aggressively fighting for It. Acting from these beliefs is a misuse of Power.

O'Sensei called for the best use of his students' neutral Power when he taught, "Mankind's role is to fulfill his heaven-sent purpose through a sincere heart that is in harmony with all creation and loves all things." In this statement, he advocated development of a peaceful Inner Presence that can diffuse conflict and build cooperation in solving the problems of today.

Clue #2: You Are Never Separate From Your Power

Misuse of Power through religion and societal conditioning has led many of us to feel disconnected from our Innate Power. Fortunately, we are never truly separate from It. We were just taught, perhaps not consciously, to shift our perception to other

"We were just taught, perhaps not consciously, to shift our perception to other people, things or events as the source of our Power, which they are not."

people, things or events as the source of our Power, which they are not. This clue helps you remember your Innate Power.

I am reminded of my Power when I experience the wonder of a butterfly dancing around me as I walk in the woods. The most amazing reminder happened when a sparrow once landed on my knee for a moment while I was relaxing on my deck watching birds drinking at the water fountain. I sense my Power as joy when I hear the wind gently playing soothing chimes and as the rush of excitement, coupled with feelings of smallness, when the wind is abruptly gusting, announcing the arrival of a storm. I notice my

"When I am giving and receiving love uncondition- ally, I am extending qualities of my Innate Power."

Power as a pulsating Magnetic Presence when being silent and still as well as when I feel sensual and creative. When I am giving and receiving love unconditionally, I am extending qualities of my Innate Power.

How do you notice your Innate Power? Have you noticed It reflected in a baby's eyes, that Magnetic Light that draws you into mimicking his or her smiles and giggles as he or she expresses amazement at the most ordinary things? Have you felt your Innate Power when awed by the beautiful artistry of nature? Have you celebrated a major accomplishment, acknowledging that it came about by more than just your personal efforts? Pause here for a moment and reflect on the many ways you have been aware of your Innate Power expressing through you and others.

Isn't it perplexing how we have these wonderful ways of experiencing our Power until some crossroads moment comes along? What happens at those times when we feel powerless or uncertain about what to do next? When we feel separate from our Power, the parts of our brain that enable us to think and make judgments about the world and people around us are translating what we see, hear, taste, smell, touch, sense, and feel based on how we have been shaped by our history. Our body is *"Our body is our Power's communication device."* our Power's communication device. Our Power hasn't gone anywhere: its device just needs a software upgrade.

We were born completely dependent upon our caregivers for survival. Whether we were loved and nurtured, neglected or abused, picked up or left to cry things out on our own, everything we went through affected our initial brain development and consequently, how we perceive the world around us. Our DNA has a software-like program that turns on at predictable intervals activating reflexes that initiate rolling over, sitting up, crawling, standing up and walking in approximately the same timeframe as everyone, unless there are complications. These movements contribute to the growth of neural fields that enable us to speak, listen, write, read and interact with things, the same systems we use to express our Innate Power.

Our Power was nurtured or masked depending upon how others modeled how to think and live, related to our playful curiosity and responded to our cries for having our needs met. By five years of age, we embodied most of our core beliefs about ourselves and the world around us. We adopted them during the time when the neocortex of our brain (its left, right and frontal lobes) was still maturing, when we lived more in our imagination.

Like a sponge, we absorbed our experiences in our mid- and hindbrain. These early sensory impressions are our source of automatic reactions to be open and curious or freeze, fight or run away.

"...early sensory impressions are our source of automatic reactions to be open and curious or freeze, fight or run away. "

As children, we acted out the behaviors of others in games and with toys, playing with and reinforcing what we saw modeled. As young adults, we started to question what we were taught and to make our own unique plans and choices, many in opposition to the wishes of our parents. For many of us, our desire to follow our hearts and go our own way was probably met with resistance. How did you respond to your upbringing? Did you comply? Did you rebel?

Isn't that how early life was for most of us? Whether we were motivated to please our parents or rebel against them, we developed a strong ego. Shaped by times gone by, our will to acquire, contribute, expose, protect, punish or reward became predominantly directed by our ego rather than by our Innate Power.

When I heard this the first time, I thought, *Who am I that is not conditioned by my upbringing? Am I just a representation of what others said or did to me?* and *Why am I here?* I eventually came to accept that we all have "histories" and that our quality of life is determined by whether we continue playing out our ego's programs or remember how to be and express our Intrinsic Wisdom.

Many gifts are seeded in childhood, whether times are difficult or easy—gifts of empathy, intuition, art, music, writing, problem-solving and more. Your parents probably didn't go to bed each night conspiring to hurt

"You align with this child-like forgiving nature and the wisdom of your Innate Power when you become grateful for the gifts you developed as a result of your upbringing."

you or mess up your life. No matter how they treated you, you probably still loved them. You align with this child-like forgiving nature and the wisdom of your Innate Power when you become grateful for the gifts you developed as a result of your upbringing. This forgiving and unconditionally loving way of being is a core quality of your Power.

You are the Curious One who knows how to forgive and love unconditionally. If you feel upset by your circumstances or uncertain about your next steps, the effects of your past have caused interference with the expression of your Innate Power. The good news is, at any time or age, you can open and grow neural fields that enable you to express all the qualities of your Innate Power.

"You are the Curious One who knows how to forgive and love unconditionally."

Clue #3: Meditation Wires Your Brain for Expressing Your Innate Power

Your brain runs your ego or your Innate Power programs. Even if the initial software is not allowing the best use of your Power, you can upgrade it. You begin to clear interference with your Power's expression when you accept what you have been given and go on the journey of uncovering the clues within the old software that lead you to the treasure of your Innate Power. You initially gain access to the clues you need by doing activities that reawaken the brain's neural fields that run your Innate Power programs. The purpose of meditation is more than quieting the mind and releasing stress, although this is a happy result as well. It is a fundamental activity that wires your

"[Meditation] is a fundamental activity that wires your brain so the systems that allow your Innate Power's expression can function optimally."

brain so the systems that allow your Innate Power's expression can function optimally.

When I studied the brain and how we learn, I realized that meditation is a physical as well as a mental exercise—sit still, relax, breathe and focus—that wires the brain so you can stop and think, rather than react. Best of all, you can practice slowing down your breathing, relaxing and shifting into your heart anywhere or anytime. When you are able to sit comfortably alone without the distractions of reading, watching television or listening to music, you have myelinated neural pathways (matured them through practice so they allow for the smooth flow of electrical impulses throughout your brain), which happens in the process of mastering any skill. Rather than impulsively reacting to people or events, meditation's neural fields support you in stopping, thinking and consciously responding because you mastered the art of sitting still with your own thoughts and feelings.

There was a time I was putting in sixty-hour workweeks. I was also in an accelerated evening master's degree program, co-raising a teenage stepson and newly elected to the board of a large church that had lost its minister and a third of its congregation. At our first board retreat, the minister who was brought in to facilitate said to us, "If you don't have time to meditate for a half hour morning and evening, then you need to meditate for an hour in the morning and an hour in the evening." "Wait a minute!" we objected and he repeated, "If there isn't time for a half hour, do it for an hour—twice a day."

Before the retreat, I had been meditating for a few minutes, most days, for about six years. Overriding resistance, I set my clock back, got up a half hour earlier and took time in the evening before bed to sit still, relax and breathe deeply. It cut into my sleep time, and yet my sleep time was more restful and rejuvenating. Six to eight hours of tossing and turning while processing my day in fitful dreams could no longer compete. My stress levels dropped dramatically and I became a kinder, more efficient and productive person when I took growing amounts of time, every day, to meditate with the intention of attuning to my Power—to, in the words of my religious upbringing, "Be still and know…" I also enjoyed some of the other benefits you will find summarized in Figure 1. I encourage you to add meditation to your routine, if you haven't already done so, and notice what it does for you. If you are already meditating an hour or more a day, indulge me as I review the benefits or feel free to jump to the next clue.

Meditating morning and evening and taking brief breaks during the day may seem difficult, initially. As you take time anyway, you too may find you have less conflict, less need to clean up mistakes and more peace, productivity and efficiency. Initially, see how meditating for five or ten minutes a couple of times a day for a week or two affects your stress. Your results will give you the incentive to continue. As you enjoy the benefits, notice what happens when you extend your meditation time to thirty or more minutes at each sitting.

Meditation Benefits

Mainstream science has studied meditation since the 1980s and found many physical, mental and emotional benefits including:

- Stress reduction
- Improved sleep time
- Lower blood pressure
- Decreased anxiety
- Increased periods of happiness
- Reduced pain
- Improved self-esteem

The latest research is summarized well by Dan Harris in one chapter of his #1 New York Times Bestseller, *10% Happier: How I Tamed The Voice In My Head, Reduced Stress Without Losing My Edge, And Found Self-Help That Actually Works—A True Story*. I enjoyed reading how a well-known television personality also found the benefits of meditation and applied them to his life.

Figure 1.

I believe in a self-empowered approach to meditating. Your Innate Power is the best source of learning to meditate. State your intention or say a little prayer affirming your desire to connect with your Power then use the following meditation protocol as a guide. Trust that the amount of time you spend is appropriate for you. Occasionally, see if you can extend the time. You have reached a nice meditation zone when you feel like you sat for ten minutes and a half an hour passed. Set an alarm so you are not concerned about time.

A Meditation Protocol

1. Sit in a comfortable position or lie down. Relax. Use relaxation sounds or music if necessary.

2. Slow down the rhythm of your breathing. For example: Breathe in for a count of 4 and out for a count of 8. Let your hands rest a couple of inches below your navel and feel your belly rise and fall with each breath.
   a. This slows down your brain wave cycle, from the thinking level of beta to the relaxed and dreamy alpha/theta levels, and slows down your heart rate.

3. Focus on any one of the following:
   a. Your breath
   b. A word or a feeling like love or peace or an uplifting phrase or melody
   c. A peaceful image

4. When you notice thoughts arise, just breathe, smile and go back to your focus.

5. Before getting up, integrate for a few moments. Smile and affirm positive beliefs about your life, such as *My life is so easy. I love my life.*

Figure 2.

Even advanced meditators have days when they are challenged to sit still with a quiet mind. If you are having difficulty relaxing and letting go of other "more urgent" priorities in your life, write them down. Before entering meditation, it helps to quiet the mind if you do some physical activity like lengthening your calves, T'ai Chi or yoga, while breathing slowly and deeply. You are training your mind to focus and be quiet, and this takes practice. There will be many opportunities to practice being patient with yourself, which enables you to be patient with others. Patience is a core quality of your Innate Power.

Clue #4: Three Steps Sustain Your Connection with Your Power

Life offers many opportunities to awaken or develop core qualities of our Innate Power. We sustain our connection with our Power as we master interrupting and upgrading ineffective early programs so, through lack of use, their neural fields become less accessible. Interrupting characteristics like worry, impatience and forcing solutions, with rest and movement breaks, allows our whole-brain functions to emerge and with them a treasure chest of gifts, including answers we seek and the peace we desire. We do this in three steps.

The first step is to notice when you have been stimulated into an ineffective habit like worry, confusion or frustration. In the second step, you apply techniques for interrupting or resolving the habit. The third step calls for you to practice a new approach. You will find techniques

Three Steps that Sustain Your Connection with Your Power

1. Notice reactive behavior.

2. Interrupt and resolve unproductive habits.

3. Practice new approaches.

Figure 3.

for building awareness, interrupting old habits and practicing new approaches throughout this guide.

Here are some examples demonstrating how to apply these steps.

Let's say you catch yourself worrying about an event that may or may not occur. First, acknowledge that you are using your mind unproductively. Next, interrupt your thoughts by doing something that gets your mind off the subject of your worry. I know a woman who detaches from worries while sewing and another while beading. Then there is my dear friend who loves to vacuum to quiet her mind. Worry is a sign that neurons are firing too much in your left brain. While focusing on a mindless activity, hum an uplifting melody to wake up your right brain. This pattern interrupt may also be your new alternative to negative futurizing.

Some office interactions can cause you to wonder if you have a left brain at all because you cannot find the words to express what you know. When you feel pressured to give a response, instead of stuttering and worrying about giving an incorrect answer, interrupt the pressure by saying, "Let me get back to you on this. I would like to think about it..." While you take a break, sip some water and do any of the brain stimulating activities you find in this guide. They are designed to switch on the parts of your brain that you need in order to think clearly and respond with authority.

Let's say you notice that you have been staring at your computer in frustration trying to problem-solve and it is not appropriate for you to leave your desk. Before you yield to the impulse to destroy your computer, sip some water and do some *Palming* to switch on your whole-brain. The few minutes you take to rest your mind will reap solutions in far less time than trying harder and harder to see what you might have missed. Let your office mates know about *Palming* so they don't interrupt you with concerns about your health.

Palming

- Let your eyes rest in your palms with your elbows on a pillow or desk while breathing slowly and deeply.

- Cup your palms and place the heel of your hand just below your eyes.

- Let your fingers rest gently on your forehead, without putting any pressure on your eyeballs.

Figure 4.

If you spend a lot of time on the computer, intermittent *Palming* can prevent the visual stress that can cause headaches, transpositions of letters or numbers and other typing and thinking errors. Visual stress is felt as dry eyes and staring coupled with shallow breathing and dry mouth. These are also symptoms of the fight/flight/freeze response in your body, which can cause you to lose touch with your need for nourishment and rest. I recommend movement or nature breaks every hour or so and sipping water frequently for healthy use of technologies.

Clue #5: Being Detached from Outcomes is a Quality of Living in Your Power

In Aikido, I was taught to detach from the outcome while intending, above all, to harmonize with and protect opponents from harm. Whenever I focused on a wrist-lock and tried hard to subdue an attacker, I would miss the escape route I had left open and find myself on the mat, instead. The same principle applies when you are wondering about your next steps. If you try really hard to figure out your options or force solutions based on what you think you should do, you can find yourself on the metaphoric mat licking your wounds, having missed what might have been revealed by letting go of the need to figure things out and taking time to be with the gap between what was and what is unfolding. There is part of a Rumi poem that reminds me of the Power of this crossroads moment: "...be a sheet of paper with nothing on it. Be a spot of ground where nothing is growing, where something might be planted, a seed possibly, from the Absolute." Out of this creative space will sprout the ability to identify your options, sit with them and notice which one speaks most emphatically to your heart.

Long before I was introduced to how I was giving my Power away, I had occasions in my life, too numerous to mention, when I relied on validation from others as my source of confidence—not to mention how many times, even now, challenges with my computer prompt me to get in touch with anger and practice patience. Take my word for it: Your Power will be given away, return, be given away and return again and again. Your footwork is noticing and acknowledging your part in what is and is not working, interrupting patterns that no longer serve you and practicing a new way. The footwork goes most easily when you approach each new awareness like an innocent child seeing something for the first time.

In Guidepost 2, you are introduced to information and activities that lay the foundation for you to develop and apply this level of innocent perception, which positions you for the best use of your Power at crossroads moments. Before making plans or taking action at your present crossroads moment, enjoy a palming or meditative moment, and relax. You will connect with your answers as you read through and do the activities in the rest of this guide.

Guidepost 2:

Develop Innocent Perception

Riding Lesson

sit calmly astride the saddle
feeling a straight line
from elbow, through reins, to bit

keep a light touch
with the horse's mouth
slack reins mean halt
stand still or
head for the barn
steady touch says
pay attention

wrap legs around belly
breathe
sit deeply
squeeze
feel the horsepower
between seat and receptive hands

a well-trained horse
responds to leg and rein cues
picks up its head
gathers its legs closer
crosses the stream

the learning-to-be-ridden
hesitates
or tries to turn and run

be
patient
persistent
and present

wrap legs around belly
breathe
sit deeply
direct head toward opposite bank
squeeze calves to ask for the crossing

> the horse places one hoof in
> brings a back leg forward
> steps in with the other front leg
> takes another step from behind
> noses the water
> blows bubbles
> paws and splashes

allow
and enjoy her play

keep a light touch
breathe
sit deeply
pay attention
be ready for the leap through
what seems fearful

> crossings
> invite the rider
> and the ridden

"When you change the way you look at things,
the things you look at change."
—Dr. Wayne Dyer

Why Mine the Treasure
in Crossroads Moments?

*B*efore my 2001 crossroads moment, my attempts at designing and living the relationship of my dreams usually ended in similar nightmares. I had a habit of losing myself in long-term relationships that eventually turned into power struggles ending in abuse or betrayal. To wake up from this cycle, my task was to become aware of how my early years were playing out in my current circumstances and walk the path of recovery. The promise of creating happy, supportive and healthy relationships—as well as a desire to heal feelings of guilt for the life my sister Jaci had led—motivated me to mine my treasure in this way.

Jaci, who was three years younger than me, made her passing at the age of forty-seven after surviving on the streets of Newport, Oregon, for nine years. Her life is a constant reminder that I, too, have been affected by alcoholism. The clues you find in this guidepost helped me view our history with clear and innocent perception—the first step towards forgiving myself and my parents, taking responsibility for my challenges and living the healthy, meaningful life I desired.

On my path, I have found that feeling victimized and blaming the past for current challenges keeps me stuck in repetitive cycles. The clues in this guidepost reveal why our best intentions can go astray and how to have them originate from our Power so we arrive at the destination we desire. This guidepost also introduces you to *Four Stages of Self-Awareness*, as I have experienced them, and clues that *Develop Innocent Perception*, so your next steps arise mindfully, from your Power.

Your riding lessons may be more or less extreme than mine. I don't know anyone who has escaped chaos, trauma or illness in their childhood. We have all formed our own unique survival patterns in relationship to these early crossroads moments. Even though they got us through difficult times and enabled most of us to function well in society, over time they can become like a comfortable old pair of shoes. We might not be able to tell or may not be willing to admit that they no longer support us, except when a pivotal crossroads moment invites us to see our denial and step out of our comfort zone shoes.

Self-awareness and acceptance point you to the treasure that you buried in the mud of growing up. Your treasure holds the answers you seek as well as the motivation, gifts and skills that will enable you to live the life you love. It is revealed when crossroads moments are viewed with innocent perception.

Clue #6: Navigating the Four Stages of Self-awareness Awakens Self-Knowledge

Innocent perception is preceded by self-awareness. It lets you view your thoughts, feelings and sensations as well as your physical, mental, emotional and spiritual needs neutrally, so you can consciously choose your responses to them. You develop and master this skill as you travel through the *Four Stages of Self-Awareness: Denial, Opening, Awakening and Mastery.*

You can find yourself at any of these stages simultaneously. For instance, you might be an expert at your work but unaware of your contribution to your relationship challenges or that your spouse or partner is unhappy with you. The Figure 5 diagram shows the progression through the stages as a gradual climb up stairs. In practice, the journey through the *Four Stages of Self-Awareness* is more a Fred Astaire/Ginger Rogers-like dance.

Four Stages of Self-Awareness

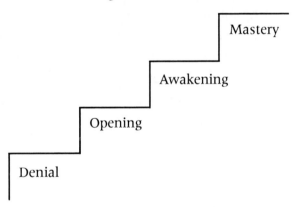

Figure 5.

Denial Stage

At the *Denial Stage*, the mindset is *I don't know what I don't know and I may or may not acknowledge that I am not interested in finding out.* I was at this stage throughout my twenties. I didn't even know that personal growth was an option. I would unknowingly self-medicate. I kept my home life a secret or lied to myself and others about what was really going on. I thought that if my hair and nails were perfect, no one at the office would notice how insecure I felt. My self-esteem was based on what I accomplished and how well-manicured I was.

Opening Stage

At the *Opening Stage,* the mindset is *I don't know what I don't know and I want to know, but I'm not sure how to find out. I seek out people and resources to help me find answers.* I opened in my early thirties, around the time I found a lump in my breast. It turned out to be a benign tumor, but the experience made me stop and question how I had been living my life. Afraid that the tumor was God's way of punishing me for perceived wrongdoings, I bargained with God, promising to dedicate my life to my spiritual path if I came through the surgery whole and alive. At this stage, I still perceived God as a punishing authority figure. My perception of God evolved as I read self-help, philosophy and spirituality books, and applied what I learned.

Awakening Stage

At the *Awakening Stage,* the mindset is *I know I am missing something. I'm not feeling as happy or satisfied as I would like to be.* I'm asking, *Is there more?, Why am I here?* and *What is my purpose?* I started asking these questions in my late thirties when I began getting conflicting feedback from my spiritual community and my then husband. My co-volunteers would rave about how smart, kind and helpful I was while at home I was used, criticized and abused. When I began to stand up for myself, he asked for a divorce, freeing me to my path of awakening. This stage led me to many healers, counselors and workshops as well as different spiritual and religious traditions.

Mastery Stage

At the *Mastery Stage*, the mindset is *I create my experience. I know that I may not know everything, that my perception may occasionally be clouded. I proactively look for clues in all my crossroads moments that reveal what I would benefit from knowing. I use those experiences to master the best use of my Power.* I have been living in this mindset for about twenty years. Yet even now, I notice moments when I resist the clues I read in my life. I know I limit my potential when I do, so I use resistance as a prompt to apply one or more of the activities or processes I present in this guide. I still use a coach. I believe it is important to have a trusted mentor who can give me a reality check because I realize how easy it is for my perception to be distorted by my history. One day at a time, I surrender to living mindfully, accepting the *Mastery Stage* as a life-long leg of my journey. Even though transforming learned beliefs and habits can sometimes be difficult, the grace I enjoy on this path is much more meaningful and fulfilling than living as I did in the first thirty-some years of my life.

Clue #7: Mindfulness Develops Innocent Perception

You have developed many parts that make up your personality. As the universe has many stars, galaxies and planets, the body many cells, bones and organs, your personality has many facets with unique ways of expressing. These parts are formed as you adopt or rebel against the beliefs and strategies of your early role models. You notice them as inner beliefs, thoughts or voices. They can sound like a controlling or encouraging parent. They can be critical of you, judgmental of others, curious, outgoing, introspective, protective and more. I name mine so as to not over-identify with them – the banker, critic, playful child, to name a few. Our personality parts are not who we are. They are how we express our Innate Power.

As you become aware of and stop identifying with the many parts of you, you are more able to choose how to respond to people and events in your life. Practicing meditation and mindfulness are tools for shifting from the perspective of your critical and judgmental parts and training your brain to be present-moment focused, where you can hear the Voice of Wisdom in you.

"Mindfulness...enables you to keep all parts of you in service to and allowing the best use of your Power."

Mindfulness—an expanded state of self-awareness—is the ability to be fully present with whatever activity or interaction you are focused on while, at the same time, being aware of your breathing, physical needs, emotional state and what is going on around you. It is a skill that enables you to keep all parts of you in service to and allowing the best use of your Power. The skill of being mindful as you do simple daily activities or make major life choices becomes accessible through practice, which develops the brain neurology that supports clear perception. (You will learn more about how to develop this skill in Clue #10.)

When you are mindful, you have access to your sixth sense, which is felt as a relaxed heart-rate, deep breathing and heightened senses. This is also how you feel when you are functioning from the best use of your Power. If you are an athlete, you may have felt like this when you were "in the zone." If you are a writer, artist or musician, you have probably felt it as a creative flow. For those who guide or work with others, you may experience it as connection, cooperation and communication that allows an easy exchange of ideas and solutions.

The Figure 6 chart is offered to help you notice how your brain allows the best use of your Innate Power. I have drawn this chart as circles within circles, graphically denoting that there is no separation between your Innate Power and the conscious and sub/unconscious parts of your mind. The message in this chart is that your sub/unconscious perspective is completely influenced by what you have stored in the middle and back systems of your brain, which telegraph messages through muscle memory, nerve channels and the voices of your parts. As you read through this chart, notice how your Innate Power and your sub/unconscious communicate through the same brain channels. For you to fully function from your Power, limiting beliefs and habits stored in the sub/unconscious must be resolved so its systems allow your Innate Power to be clearly expressed.

"For you to fully function from your Power, limiting beliefs and habits stored in the sub/unconscious must be resolved so its systems allow your Innate Power to be clearly expressed."

Innate Power
- Detected when the back, middle, right and frontal brain systems function together, allowing access to an intuitive sixth sense
- Its language is symbol, metaphor, energy, feeling and sensation
- It is experienced as a gentle, wise, felt sense of peace and knowing, with relaxed physical functions

Conscious Perspective
- Relies only on information from the five senses: touch, taste, smell, sight and hearing
- Uses mostly left brain functions: logical, rational, analytical and detail-oriented
- Discounts right and frontal brain functions: instinctual, big picture, rhythm, tone, visionary and altruistic expressions
- Its language is mostly verbal: mental chatter and talking a lot
- It is experienced as willpower

Sub/Unconscious Perspective
- Its prime directive is survival
- Noticed as the back brain reflex to freeze or the middle brain reflex to fight or run
- Sensed through the body's autonomic functions (heartbeat, breath, thirst, sweat, hormones, etc.)
- Its language is symbol, metaphor, energy, feeling and sensation
- It is experienced as unconscious reactions and intense emotions

Figure 6.

Clue #8: Your Brain Runs a Program
Called the Projection Dilemma

The primary obstacle I have met while traveling through the *Four Stages of Self-Awareness*—that everyone meets when they are struggling—is a belief program I call the *Projection Dilemma*. Kept hidden, the *Projection Dilemma* eventually sabotages any life endeavor. As you become aware of when you or others are in the *Projection Dilemma*, your role is not to blame, criticize, fix or excessively analyze yourself or them. It is to allow and affirm what rings true as you unlearn ways of thinking and behaving that no longer serve you.

The Projection Dilemma

We all react or respond based on our own unique perception. We take in experiences through all our senses. The brain compares real-time sights, sounds, smells and sensations to the history files stored in the deepest parts of our brain. From that information, we form a judgment and project that thought onto the current situation. Then we respond, based upon our projection and interpretation.

In other words, when interacting with someone whose words, body language and/or tone of voice sound or look like a person from your past—and you react using strategies that kept you safe back then—it is as if you are seeing through the eyes of your childhood template, mistaking the person in front of you for the one in the past. If a chaotic current event has a similar feel to a childhood one and you react as you did back then, you have dropped into your sub/unconscious perspective, which operates outside of time and misperceives the current situation as the past. For example, a mom I know said recently, "I feel like I have recreated my family chaos." She may be right. We usually do unless we resolve our wounds.

However, this mom is learning that it may only be a shift in perspective that would enable her to discern chaos from the many dynamics of raising children. This shift is happening as she makes her way through the *Four Stages of Self-Awareness.*

Picture a person with an old movie projector as a head, like the one in Figure 7. You are in the *Projection Dilemma* when, without being aware of it, you project memories of difficult times on the screen of current situations, reacting to present circumstances as if they were the past.

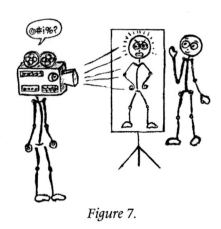

Figure 7.

Contemplate the person who never says good morning, who walks in looking at the floor or races quickly to get their coffee. Is it that they don't like you or could it be that they are focused on a deadline and their lack of interaction has nothing to do with you?

Are you the person who makes getting your coffee a more urgent matter than saying good morning, thinking you will get your work done faster if you are not distracted? You are also making this determination based on your perception of the situation, which may or may not be accurate. How you interpret situations and the actions of others drives your behavior.

If your buttons are getting pushed at crossroads moments, there is something about the person or event that reminds you— usually below your conscious awareness—of an unresolved past experience that when resolved will allow you to find the ability to respond with clarity and confidence. When I shared the *Projection Dilemma* with a wise friend, she summarized it nicely: "Projection equals perception."

Your ability to see with innocent perception arises when you recognize that everyone wears a projector on their head, much of the time. Awareness of *Projection Dilemma* dynamics puts you in a position of choice, which is a quality of living in your Power. You may choose to continue projecting your beliefs and feelings onto others and reacting to your projections or stop projecting and accept responsibility for upgrading this behavior. Others may never admit that they are projecting. Yet, when you become aware of when you are and see—with innocent perception—how their behavior or way of communicating is not causing your reaction, it will be easier to look past their behaviors or mannerisms and build rapport, work or live in harmony with them.

My intention for exposing the *Projection Dilemma* is to inspire compassion for why people talk and act the way they do and help you step from the *Opening,* through the *Awakening* and into the *Mastery Stage.* Within the *Mastery Stage* is the potential for your own *Projection Dilemma's* resolution.

Clue #9: Accept Before Taking Action or You May Wish You Took a Different Path

When you first become aware of the *Projection Dilemma*, it is natural to want to do something to prevent it, make amends for or overcome it. As admirable as these desires are, they too can be driven by projected guilt.

There is an interim step before taking action: acceptance. When you get your buttons pushed—which indicates you are in the *Projection Dilemma*—being with what you think and feel for a day or more, before taking action, is recommended. Using the time to write about the situation or discuss it with a trusted advisor helps you to resolve your own discomfort before acting. Practicing acceptance is not throwing up your hands and venting, "It is what it is!" It does not mean condoning inappropriate behavior or avoiding difficult decisions. Acceptance makes space for you to calm down and gather your thoughts, so you can interact and problem-solve proficiently.

For now, affirm *awareness and acceptance before action*. You will get better results than with prematurely asking for a change in behavior, offering a verbal apology or taking action. Remember, it is not so much what you do as who you are becoming on your journey. You will have many opportunities to take whatever actions you deem best. By gleaning the wisdom at each guidepost, your decisions will arise more from the best use of your Power than from what may presently be a distorted perception.

"Remember, it is not so much what you do as who you are becoming on your journey."

Clue #10: Mindfulness Begins the Projection Dilemma's Undoing

My time on the Aikido mat taught me that one of the greatest means for diffusing an attacker is to be aware of his or her strategies, both subtle and obvious. Playing the adversary role called for me to practice new behaviors, helping me understand an opponent's mentality in a way no words could approach. Being on the receiving end of a strike taught me how to take an opponent's point of view and harmonize with their movement, throw or subdue them. One day while practicing Aikido, I became mindful that I was standing in my father's shoes and undoing behaviors he had taught me. This seeded compassion and a greater motivation for overcoming my challenges.

Mindfulness prepares you to engage, adapt to or leave unhealthy situations by enabling you to more easily catch yourself when you fall into the *Projection Dilemma* and manage your response when others seem to be in theirs. Many times, it circumvents chal-

"Many times, [mindfulness] circumvents challenges before they occur because your reflexes are not in charge of your decisions and actions."

lenges before they occur because your reflexes are not in charge of your decisions and actions.

Begin to cultivate mindfulness by consciously noticing your thoughts, feelings and body sensations before, during and after activities and conversations. Start with simple activities for a couple of weeks, like those found in the Figure 8 *Tips for Developing Innocent Perception*. This begins to create a new habit. When you are able to be mindful while doing the dishes or exercising, you create physical changes in your brain that lay the foundation for allowing the same attention with more challenging people and situations.

Tips for Developing Innocent Perception

1. Be mindful and curious.
   a. Notice, as a baby who sees a colorful new toy, what you are thinking, feeling and sensing, positive or negative.
      i. Are your thoughts peaceful or worrisome, creative or limited?
      ii. Are you feeling glad, sad, angry or afraid, or a variation on one of these emotions?
      iii. Notice your breathing and the muscle tension around your jaw, shoulders, spine and the backs of your legs. Notice if you are blinking or staring, hungry or tired.
   b. Describe inwardly or out loud what you are doing. *I am washing the dishes...listening to children laugh...laughing inwardly with them...*

(continued next page)

2. Break routines and establish new ones.
   a. Be mindful as you occasionally drive a different route
      to work or take other transportation.
   b. Vary your breakfast, lunch or dinner menu. Focus on
      eating only—no speaking, reading or watching
      television. Notice your thoughts, feelings and digestion
      as you eat, and for the hour following a meal.
   c. Instead of watching TV or being on the computer one
      night, study the growth of plants or the activities of
      birds in the evening light.

3. Take up a whole-body movement activity like T'ai Chi, yoga,
   dance, swimming or walking in nature. Be mindful as you do it.

4. Acknowledge awareness.
   a. Teach your inner critic to say *Good noticing!* instead of
      Look how you messed up again! Without awareness, there
      would be no ability to change.

5. Keep a journal and record what you did or did not notice as
   you review your day. Reflect on your contribution to difficulties.
   a. How might you have contributed to the situation?
      i.   What emotional state were you in?
      ii. What thoughts were you thinking at the time?
      iii. What was your body language like?
   b. What would you do differently the next time?
   c. Do you need assistance from a coach, mentor or
      support group?

6. Unwrap the gifts.
   a. Notice and record what's different in your response or
      the reactions of others to any changes in your approach.
   b. Acknowledge new ideas or renewed interest in
      creative activities.

Figure 8.

Clue #11: The Projection Dilemma is a Misuse of Your Imagination

After using the *Tips for Developing Innocent Perception* to explore how challenges at the dojo (the martial art training studio) were inviting me to reconnect with my Power, I realized that getting injured and having too many close calls, as I tested for higher and higher levels of achievement, was a result of not listening to a quiet, yet persistent inner voice suggesting it was time for me to meet another sensei. My history would have found me staying loyal to the rules and authority figure of the dojo even if, intuitively, I knew it was time to move on. Acknowledging and accepting my awareness that my time was complete there, without judging myself or my sensei, allowed me to embrace the lessons and take action with positive intent. I was able to discuss my decision with him and remain friends as I broke my "rules" and left his dojo.

The *Projection Dilemma* is a misuse of your imagination. Your ego is imagining that the present is actually the past and sending you physical, mental and emotional signals so you act as if it is. The results you get when you or others are functioning in the *Projection Dilemma* are about as good as traveling the ocean with a broken compass, not knowing how to read the stars. As you *Develop Innocent Perception*, incidences of the *Projection Dilemma* decrease and your ability to perceive accurately returns. The next guidepost provides additional clues that give you growing access to conscious use of your imagination—the insightful, skilled and creative true north within you.

Guidepost 3:
Consciously Use Your Imagination

When

standing outside the whitewashed arena
no taller than father's knee
watching horses and riders trot and canter at his command
imagining the horse between your legs

>   you knew you could ride

>   when

sitting astride your pony outside the Cow Palace arena
grandstands filled with rustling friends and parents
rehearsing turns and clear flights over fences
wondering if your pony was big enough

>   you won blue ribbons

>   when

hugging your pony in her dark wooden stall
silently crying
whispering secrets
telling not allowed

>   you shared your pain

>   when

imaging the lives of your future children
afraid a dire outcome loomed
rejecting motherhood
wanting to know your purpose

>   you birthed careers

when

picturing the initials V.P. behind your name
you inflated your experience
longing for recognition
fearing you'd be found out

    you achieved your goal

    when

wanting to love again
he danced into your life
seeing his potential
denying your own

    he betrayed you

    when

desires unveil shadows
surrender your agenda
sit silently inside an inner smile
knowing the truth

    shadows signal the direction of Light

"Imagination is your preview of life's coming attractions."
"Imagination is more important than knowledge."
—Albert Einstein

"Live out of your imagination, not your history."
—Stephen Covey

Consciously Attract What You Want

*O*ur imagination is the source of all we create. Structures, cities, money, technologies and children were all first held in someone's imagination. Before we landed our job(s) or found the love(s) of our life, we imagined them—albeit, for many of us, not consciously. When we make the connection between our *Projection Dilemma* motivated actions and the experiences we have in our life, we gain access to the ability to consciously attract or create what we desire.

This guidepost introduces additional clues that reveal how *Projection Dilemma* beliefs that exist outside of your conscious awareness affect what you imagine and project onto other people or situations. You will connect with how your language telegraphs those beliefs and affects your state of balance. As you read, reflect on how the crossroads moment that brought you to this guide might have been influenced by those beliefs. Before exiting this guidepost, I show you how to switch on your brain so you can shift *Projection Dilemma* imaginings into accurate present-time perceptions, access the most constructive powers of your imagination and create what you truly desire.

Clue #12: Out of Your Use of Awareness Comes All that You Experience

Midway through my banking career, I met with a pivotal crossroads moment. I was given the opportunity to make a presentation to my peers and froze. I could not say my name in front of a group of fifteen managers, and I couldn't hold my hand still enough to sip water. Later, as I sat tearful and embarrassed in front of my boss, worried that my career was over at twenty-eight, I fired fear as my decision-maker and committed to doing whatever it took to build my self-confidence and self-esteem. This decision led me on what, at times, seemed like detours in my life. In truth, it took me more directly to the treasure I desired.

For a long time after making my promise, I still resisted the idea that what I imagined about speaking to audiences was causing my symptoms of fear. I held to my *Projection Dilemma* belief that, without a doubt, the audience was causing my reactions. Wishing things were different, blaming my troubles on others and feeling as if I were a victim of circumstances when I was unable to control my nervousness was keeping me stuck in the very condition I committed to overcoming. It wasn't until I finally accepted the idea that my sub/unconscious beliefs and imaginings were causing my experience that I made significant progress in transforming my fear.

Your crossroads moment is presenting you with an opportunity to recognize that your use of awareness is driving your results. If you want to design and create a different outcome, your crossroads moment is also inviting you to build on your understanding of the *Projection Dilemma* by connecting its influence to your present experiences. Once you

"Your crossroads moment is presenting you with an opportunity to recognize that your use of awareness is driving your results."

see and feel this connection, you will learn to apply tools (which will be introduced later in this guide) that help you shift your perception. On this leg of your treasure hunt, you discover how much Power you truly have by remembering how your thoughts create your experience. Here's how:

What you believe about what you perceive directs your imagination. What you imagine fuels your feelings, which drive your actions, which create your outcomes.

Awareness ➔ Belief ➔ Imagination ➔ Feeling ➔ Action ➔ Outcome

Take my crossroads moment in front of my peers. The truth is, my *awareness* of being in front of this audience triggered my sub/unconscious *belief—I'm not safe here.* My *imagination*, running memories of when it wasn't okay for me to speak up, flooded me with *feelings* of fear, concurrently switching on neural fields causing my *action*—to freeze. The *outcome* was that I was unable to make the presentation. My supervisor took over and did it for me. I created freezing in front of the audience because of an inaccurate present-moment perception.

I didn't know then what I know now, so within six months while deep in my *Denial Stage*, I followed the man in my life six hundred miles north to Seattle. (My Self-editing parts motivated me to get away and delay looking at myself.) Within the first year at the next bank, I found myself sitting at a boardroom table making loan recommendations to senior executives. Speaking with this group of men was just as intimidating as the time I froze, yet for some reason, I had greater self-control when sitting down. Afraid of repeating the past, I took my former boss's advice and joined Toastmasters soon thereafter. When, decades later, I accepted that I was the source of my results and decided to address my *Projection Dilemma* habits, I had made it through my *Opening Stage* and into my *Awakening Stage*. Now, nervousness doesn't cripple me. Even with some butterflies in my stomach, I can talk without losing my train of thought, breathe deeply and resolve any anxiousness as I speak. Participants in my seminars and workshops even say I am quite an engaging and inspirational speaker.

Clue #13: Clear Perception is Not Irreparably Affected by the Projection Dilemma

Clear perception returns as you learn to notice when you are out of balance, have knowledge of how to function in balance and give your brain and body the nutrients and activities they need to function optimally.

**Three Steps
to Clear Perception**

1. Know when you are out of balance.

2. Know how to function in balance.

3. Take care of your brain and body.

Figure 9.

When You Are Out of Balance

Whenever you worry or spend too much left-brain dominant time without a break, like working more than a couple of hours at a time on a computer or repetitively going over your bank statement, manuscript or HTML code without seeing the error, you can easily fall into the *Projection Dilemma*. Access to the resolution powers of your

imagination is blocked whenever you are driven to continue—
after many hours of research—certain that the answer is just
one more click away, until you find yourself back where you
started, with the problem yet unsolved.

Thinking too much or mindlessly following routines is one
way you avoid feeling your feelings while inaccurately imagining
that you have control over your life. Your ability to plan each step
of a marketing plan or new stops on a vacation, pay bills or figure
out how to afford the car of your dreams are valuable skills and
yet when they become ends in themselves, they can keep you
from the treasure you seek.

A former instructor of mine often said, "The eyes alone are
incapable of seeing the vision that all the
senses together are capable of
seeing." She related a study
done with members of a
third world tribe that, when
shown a snapshot of a mountain, could

*"The eyes alone are incapable
of seeing the vision that all the
senses together are capable
of seeing."*

not see it. Apparently, they had not developed the neural fields
necessary for focusing on and interpreting a two-dimensional image.
Another study she described was done with cats. One set was raised in
an environment of all horizontal structures and the other in an
environment of all vertical structures. When they switched the cats
from their home to the other environment, they would run into objects
because they couldn't see them. Whenever you disagree with someone
and take a fixed position that your ideas are right and the opinions of
others are wrong, you are not unlike the cats or the third world tribe.

Watching too much television or online programming
contributes to mental and emotional imbalances. Along with
negative commercial and program content, frequent light and scene
changes can cause you to stare and hold your breath. This tells your
unconscious mind that it is not safe, which triggers all sorts of fight,

flight or freeze responses: dry eyes, thirst, holding your breath, drowsiness, interrupted sleep cycles, muscle tension, grinding teeth and emotional reactivity, to name a few.

Being out of balance is a crossroads moment.

When You Are In Balance

The experience of balance is a process of self-discovery that is unique to each person. Consider the following indicators of living in balance as you discover what it is for you.

Your mental, emotional and physical systems are in balance when you think you are certain, yet remain open; you can genuinely hear another person's point of view, even if you disagree; you care more about helping people feel heard, understood and valued, than being right; you can stop, reflect and choose a different approach, instead of continually forcing solutions; decision-making is easy; you have the ability to focus, concentrate and keep your perspective at the same time; you are experiencing synchronicities and positive outcomes; you are consciously varying doing and being, work and rest, repetitive and creative activities; and when crossroads moments find you reflecting on your deeper desires and exploring how to realize them.

Take Care of Your Brain and Body

You lay the foundation for clear perception when you balance mental activities with whole-body movement, quality nourishment and rest. Consciously breathing while exercising, healthy snacks and balanced meals that include protein, carbohydrates and good fat give your brain the nutrients it needs to function optimally. It is important to stop feeding your unconscious mind negativity and fear and control what you allow into it, especially when waking up in the morning and going to sleep at night. During these times, your brain cycle is slowing from the neocortex level of beta through the more receptive middle and back brain cycles of alpha and theta, before reaching the sleep cycle of delta. These are the best times to turn off your electronics and record harmonious beliefs and feelings by meditating, using affirmations, listening to peaceful music or reading something inspirational. During waking hours, the *Activities that Switch on Your Whole-brain* (pages 73 and 74) can be used for returning to balance at any time.

Clue #14: Your Language Telegraphs Your Beliefs and State of Balance

I address communication strategies in more depth in *Guidepost 6: Your Communication Toolkit*. This clue touches on four skills that help you notice when you are out of balance and enable you to return to and stay in balance: using power-packed words and phrases, being conscious of how you follow the words "I am...", substituting "Yes and..." for "Yeah but..." and saying "Yes" when you mean *Yes* and "No" when you mean *No*.

Power-packed Words and Phrases

Phrases riddled with shoulds and have-tos are signals that you are out of balance. These and similar words echo your *Projection Dilemma* beliefs and feelings. Remember, what you believe feeds your imagination which eventually creates your outcomes. When you follow I with words like can't, don't, must, should, have to, need to and ought to, or use generalizations like always and never, it sounds as if other forces are in charge of your life. Power-packed words and phrases acknowledge that you are in charge of your response to outside influencers. They sound like I can, have, will, choose to, get to, look forward to and would like to or state specific facts. With them, you program beliefs that originate from your Power. Notice how it feels to say "I have to..." or "I need to go to work" compared to "I choose to go to work today" or "I am going to work now because of all the benefits my family and I receive." Play with this for a few days and notice how using the empowered language affects your level of enthusiasm and serenity as well as the overall quality of your day.

I Am

Beginning a statement with "I am..." can be either empowering or disempowering depending on what follows. Saying "I am" affirms who you are and what you believe. For instance, saying "I am trying" in

"Saying 'I am' affirms who you are and what you believe."

frustration affirms that you are struggling to do something without much success. Did you ever receive "Try harder" messages when you were at an impressionable young age? (I remember getting this message when I was stumbling over words as I read aloud in fifth grade. I felt like I was never going to get it, which contributed to my fear of speaking.) Saying "I am trying" can bring up memories as well as the resulting self-esteem issues and feelings you developed. "I am doing my best" is a nice substitute that affirms you are giving your best effort when you are unable to honestly say "I can" or "I will do that." I find that inviting others to do their best reduces the performance pressures they put on themselves and enhances their results. Another example is expressing "I am worried", which creates an empathetic identification with things that may or may not occur, making it easier to endlessly obsess about worst-case scenarios. Factually stating "I am thinking about... and feeling concerned that..." is an approach that affirms your choice to think and feel a certain way.

Yes And Versus Yeah But

If you have ever objected, "Yeah but...", you contributed to any imbalance that may have arisen in an exchange. Notice how you and others use "Yeah but..." to interrupt, force an opinion or hurry things along. When you are in

"A Yes and attitude helps you acknowledge an ineffective exchange and create a time when both parties can bring their best to a dialogue."

balance, you express a *Yes and* attitude: "Yes, I want to hear your ideas and I would like to schedule a time when I can give you the attention you deserve." Let's say you are confronted with a "Yeah but..." when you share your concerns and ideas. Instead of compounding an imbalanced exchange by reacting with "Yeah but I'm not finished", a *Yes and* response might sound like "That's an interesting perspective; let's schedule a time to discuss this further." A *Yes and* attitude helps you acknowledge an ineffective exchange and create a time when both parties can bring their best to a dialogue.

Yes or No

Do you say "Yes" when you mean *Yes* and "No" when you mean *No*? Or do you beat around the bush, hinting at what you mean, expecting people to read your mind? I am becoming more comfortable with being direct as I learn to communicate from my Power. My greatest challenge has been eliminating the need to justify my position when all that is necessary is a simple "Yes, I can do that", "No, that doesn't work for me" or "I don't know; let me find out." When in our Power, we don't feel the need to justify ourselves although we might choose to offer an explanation if it will enhance understanding or a relationship.

The Power of Potent Language

Optimistic language makes your tone of voice and body language resound positively and lets others know that you value their ideas, even if you disagree with them. Negative language triggers your imagination to focus on what you don't want—the result being, you get more of what you don't want. This downward spiral is demonstrated in the experience of a former manager talking about life after being downsized out of an organization and painting an effortful picture of networking unsuccessfully for a new job. Her tone of voice was worrisome as she said, "I have to get a job. I am afraid of getting another one like the last one. I don't know why it is so hard." She had been unable to find a new income stream for a year.

Even though she felt a compelling need to work, I encouraged her to set aside plenty of time before her next interview for gratefully reflecting on what she had accomplished, assessing which skills she would like to bring to the next position and resolving her anger and grief over being rejected. I suggested that she invest this time in upgrading her state of mind so she might authentically affirm "I have valuable skills and ideas to share. Every interview gets me closer to the company that is looking for my skills and expertise. I prepare and do my best in each interview." She agreed when I asked "Would you feel greater personal Power? Do you think you might see more possibilities and significantly increase your chances of getting what you want?"

The practice of communicating with potent language challenges sub/unconscious perceptions. Sometimes your inner critic will attempt to deny the truth of positive language by making it difficult for you to change your approach. Positive beliefs and words arise naturally and authentically the more you interrupt your self-defeating language patterns and practice speaking affirmatively.

I have learned that retraining myself flows most smoothly when I approach the process with a gentle and playful

"Positive beliefs and words arise naturally and authentically the more you interrupt your self-defeating language patterns and practice speaking affirmatively."

attitude—with innocent perception—as I listen to and adjust how I talk about what I plan, what I am doing and what I have done. The reward is a happy or productive interchange of ideas and collaboration in problem solving.

Clue #15: Imagination and Play are Innate Intelligences

It is through imaginary play that we develop our potential for tolerance, compassion and understanding. Children who are nurtured in a safe environment and allowed the freedom to use their imagination in playtime do not grow up to be violent; among other reasons, they have developed the brain structures that enable them to choose alternatives to fighting. Playing alone and with playmates, our imaginary games laid the foundation for future times when we might be called on to resolve differences, invent new products or systems or come up with solutions to family, community, ecological and humanitarian issues. Play and imagination are innate intelligences that let us build on what is known and discover previously unknown solutions. This process of improving on the past is how we evolve and progress.

"Play and imagination are innate intelligences that let us build on what is known and discover previously unknown solutions. This process of improving on the past is how we evolve and progress."

If effectively using your imagination is elusive or you don't trust it, you are not alone. Perhaps you didn't have the benefit of a parent reading to you or the freedom to play independently when you were young. Perhaps you heard one too many times, "It is just your imagination" or "Stop staring out the window and pay attention." If you are uncomfortable with your active imagination, you, too, are not alone. Maybe you didn't have a safe and stable way to confirm what you were seeing or sensing or learn how to persuade people to see from your perspective. Self-criticism, lack of self-trust and overriding your imagination are symptoms of having been criticized for sharing things you saw or heard, that others could not see or hear.

Learned habits, compounded by a lack of balance between mental and emotional states and physical nourishment, is underpinning *Projection Dilemma* responses such as reacting defensively, having difficulty putting your words on paper and holding back saying or doing what is in your heart. Regardless, it is possible to build or unleash your imagination's visual, auditory and sensory potential at any age. Imagination led your play when you were young. The neural fields are already there, ready to be used or reawakened at any time. It is like getting back on a bicycle after many years and you can still ride. Just using it brings it back. The following activities are reminders of how to reconnect with your wonderful imagination:

"...it is possible to build or unleash your imagination's visual, auditory and sensory potential at any age."

Activities for
Awakening Your Imagination

1. Imagine an inner smile in your heart, on your forehead and cheeks, behind your eyes and in every cell of your body while going about your day.

2. Stroll in nature, appreciating its beauty.

3. Play imagination games with friends or your children. Let your children be your teachers.

4. Go on a silent retreat during which you get away from routines and technologies.

5. Do something fun and artistic. Read or write poetry. Draw. Doodle. Arrange flowers or sculpt bushes. Knit. Sew. Play a musical instrument.

6. Laugh, for no reason other than to laugh.

Figure 10.

Clue #16: Innate Intelligences Awaken When You Balance Your Brain

The mind-body field I embraced after leaving my banking career taught me how to live in what my teachers called a whole-brain way of being. I experienced that when I functioned in a whole-brain way, all parts of my brain cooperatively interacted allowing my Innate Power qualities—playful curiosity, vulnerability, creativity, forgiveness and unconditional love, to name a few—to express. It also helped me have better balance, coordination, focus and concentration, and to more easily say or write what I was thinking. When I was out of balance or struggling, I learned to stop what I was doing and do activities that stimulated more of my brain. As a preventative measure, I learned to occasionally throughout the day do targeted mind-body activities designed to stimulate neural fields throughout my brain and heart. Balancing mental activities with movement breaks helps me be creative and playful in my approach to life.

Whenever I feel out of balance, I expand on step two of the *Three Steps that Sustain Connection with Your Power* (page 29) by doing one or more of the following Figure 11 *Activities that Switch on Your Whole-brain*. For instance, in Step #1 I might notice that I am holding my breath, staring and thinking too much when I am working on the computer. This self-awareness would lead me to take Step 2, where I blink, breathe, lengthen my calves and go for a walk so I stimulate the creative and intuitive parts of my brain. I know this shift has happened when my breathing is deeper and my perspective expands, worries dissolve or thoughts become more optimistic. If my imbalance was triggered by a public speaking event, I would take Step 3 and create as much stage time as possible so being in front of groups feels natural.

Whenever you are trying to no avail; when words aren't flowing; when you are holding your breath, gritting your teeth, thinking too much, being too dramatic and emotional or out of touch with your feelings, take a break and do some of the Figure 11 *Activities that Switch on Your Whole-brain*. These crossroads moments are opportunities to stop reinforcing old habits. Balancing your brain is a way of living in your Power and a step toward initiating new ones.

It can be as easy as gently blinking, taking a deep breath, slowly breathing out and relaxing as you lift your eyes from this page and, while continuing to breathe slowly and deeply, looking to the horizon as you observe what your peripheral vision reveals. Pause for a moment and do this activity. Did you notice how your thoughts and feelings changed and you relaxed? You can consciously choose to adjust how you think and feel that simply. Even better, you can be proactive and do activities that switch on your brain when you get up in the morning, before you begin a project, take a test or putt a ball—whenever you want to feel more balanced, focused, creative and in your Power.

Activities that Switch on Your Whole-brain

1. Sip water.

   a. Water is the first chemical that initiates all other chemical reactions in the body. It is essential for healthy brain and body functioning. Water provides fresh oxygen to your brain cells and conducts the electrical energy across synapses connecting neural fields, giving you access to a greater context and/or ability to see detail. Water's oxygen molecules get absorbed through the mucus membranes in your mouth. Sipping throughout the day, rather than sporadically gulping large volumes of water, delivers more of its oxygenating qualities to your brain while minimizing toilet breaks.

2. Breathe deeply and slowly.

   a. Let life-giving oxygen bathe your cells.

   b. Relaxed, deep breathing causes your brain waves to slow from the conscious thinking, beta brain state to the creative, intuitive alpha and meditative theta brain states, where you connect with your imagination.

   c. Be mindful of breathing deeply as you do activities throughout the day.

3. Do movements that stimulate neural fields throughout your brain.

   a. Do *Palming* (pictured on page 31).

   b. Yawn and rub your TMJ points (about an inch in front of your ear where you feel your jaw hinge as you open your mouth to yawn).

   c. Lengthen your calf muscles by doing a "runner's stretch."

   d. Sitting in a chair, twist your spine and relax into the turn for a moment in each direction.

   e. Walk, letting both arms swing fully and naturally. As you walk, look up at the tops of trees; look down at the street near your toes and out to the distant horizon; keep your head straight ahead and look, with just your eyes, at all you can see to your left; do the same looking to your right; then, imagine a circle in front of you as you walk and slowly focus on the details of everything that the circumference touches, first clockwise then counterclockwise; add looking back and forth, like when reading, being sure to focus on what you see along the spectrum from one side to the other.

   f. Stand, sit or lie down. Lift your right knee and touch it with your left hand, return to your starting position, then lift your left knee and touch it with your right hand. Add the eye movements, described in 3.e. for more brain stimulation. For more stomach area muscle activation, touch your elbow to your knee instead of your hand.

   g. Sip water during and after doing brain-stimulating activities. Also, remember to breathe deeply as you do eye and whole-body movement activities.

Figure 11.

Reading is mostly a mental activity. Pause here for a moment and switch on your whole-brain power by doing some of the activities listed in Figure 11. Pick the ones that you like most. Continue doing the activities for a minute or two. Notice and appreciate how things are different when you return to reading or move on to your next project.

Clue #17: Shadows Signal the Direction of Light

Studying and applying mind-body processes and techniques led me to develop a strong respect for the shadow parts of my mind and their effects on my self-esteem, ability to express myself and confidence to live the life I love. I found worrisome imaginings elicited uncomfortable emotional and physical symptoms, misunderstandings and reactive behaviors. Peaceful imaginings elicited thoughtful responses, courage, gratitude, new gifts, synchronous events and a desire to help others.

Developing awareness, changing your language, taking charge of what you put into your mind and activating your whole-brain power prepare you to stop living from shadowy programs that drive the *Projection Dilemma*. Coupled with allowance and a little help where needed, you, too, can have lasting changes in attitude, feeling and behavior.

Einstein is credited for defining insanity as "...doing the same thing over and over and expecting different results." Each time I held back speaking or surrendered to a negative status quo, I reinforced my shadow's neurology. Then when a job or relationship ended, the next one turned out to be no more than a variation on the theme of the previous one. Everywhere I went, there I was using shadow-driven strategies while struggling with similar challenges.

The cycle of struggle begins to break down when you start viewing it as just another crossroads moment inviting you to review your life and consciously design the one you would love. I have learned that this is not about putting in more effort. In the process of surrendering the need to struggle, you, too, may find that you are building a peaceful platform from which your creative potential can fully emerge. By embracing crossroads moments for discovering and expressing your own unique potential, life can become a daily adventure of awakening awareness, upgrading beliefs and how you use your imagination, listening to and giving healthy expression to all parts of yourself, and acknowledging progress.

Each crossroads moment is inviting you to contemplate, *What would I like to create for my tomorrows?* Guidepost 4, coming up next, guides you to design, clarify or reaffirm what *you*, free of *Projection Dilemma* imaginings, might desire. Subsequent guideposts provide the information and more resources that assist you in fulfilling your desires.

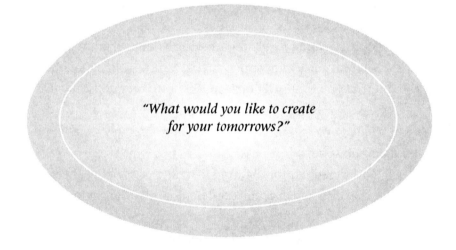

"What would you like to create
for your tomorrows?"

Guidepost 4:
Map Your Authentic Desires

Begin

You never know
what's possible
until you
begin.

> giggly baby
> falls forward
> with wobbly confidence
> into its first steps
> not knowing or even caring
> if the ground will catch his feet

Fall into
blank canvases
beckoning pages
and unbroken ground.

Smile at the horizon
and the unknown expanse
in between
lean forward
begin.

> picked up on arrival
> thrown in the air
> screaming hugs
> wiggling back down
> so excited to walk again

You never know
what's possible
until you
begin.

"Then I asked: Does a firm persuasion that a thing is so make it so? He replied: All poets believe that it does, and in ages of imagination this firm persuasion removed mountains; but many are not capable of a firm persuasion of anything."
—William Blake, *The Marriage of Heaven and Hell*

Clue #18: Your Treasure Map Guides Your Tomorrows

*T*his guidepost assists you in developing your own personal treasure map outlining what you would like to create for your tomorrows. Before you read on, you may want to pause here for a moment and revisit your original intention and the circumstances that attracted you to this guide, which you wrote on page 2. Were you assimilating a major life event, confused about your next steps? Were you frustrated with your results, feeling powerless or struggling in some other way? How you feel about your original intention can change as you become more aware of how your sub/unconscious may be viewing your present crossroads moment(s). If how you framed your original intention is different now, acknowledge yourself by updating it. This anchors the growth you have enjoyed thus far and prepares you to enter this guidepost fresh and open to creating your next steps from your Innate Power.

"When you write responses to each of the sections that follow, you set into motion the Power of putting your dreams on paper."

When you write your responses to each of the sections that follow, you set into motion the Power of putting your dreams on paper.

You will get the best results when you approach this activity in a meditative way, with the intention of connecting with your heartfelt desires. Let your treasure map guide your decision to either accept and be happy with or become a catalyst for change in your present circumstances, or let it direct your way to something new.

The components that will make up your treasure map and the activities that will help you develop it arose out of my business banking team's roller coaster ride through five reorganizations in the two-year timeframe before my exit and my experience of becoming a mind-body coach after leaving. You will find an overview of the map in Figure 12 on page 84. It is followed by specific directions for developing each of its components: *Purpose, Mission, Core Values, Vision, Goals* and *Action Steps*. Before jumping into developing your treasure map, go with me on the journey that seeded its creation and the unique approach to its application.

Several times as the bank downsized, merged or reorganized, the leaders asked us to get our teams on board with the bank's latest mission statement. The third time, my team members pushed back saying, "What's the point? They don't care about us; why should we care about them? What about those who got laid off? What if we're next?"

One morning a few days after I met with resistance from my team, I took them off site and let them vent. When they were complete, instead of telling them to park it at the door and get to work, I asked them to indulge me in a discussion about mission statements. I started with, "What's the purpose of a mission statement?" Everyone agreed that leaders use them to establish their brand image, as well as a unified focus on products, services and intended results and companies integrating them are more successful than those that don't. Then I asked, "If it works for businesses, why not for us? Instead of feeling like puppets with the bank pulling our strings, what if we identified our own personal mission statement, so we proactively participate in the changes knowing that they are helping us to fulfill our own mission?"

Since I had listened to and validated their concerns, they were open to thinking about this. To further emphasize the personal benefits of doing their own mission statement, I addressed their concerns directly: "Let's say you lose your job. What are your options? Do you go to the next organization and say, 'I got downsized out and I am looking for a job.' Or, do you say to the interviewer, 'I come to you from an organization that went through many changes in a short timeframe. In the process of making the best of it, I discovered my own mission and reaffirmed my values. I notice your company has a similar mission and similar values. That is why I am knocking on your door.'" Then I asked them, "Who would you hire?" "Who would you keep?" and "How would it help you start your own business, if you choose to go that way?" They understood the power of the latter option and opened to engaging current events from their Power.

The process of writing a personal mission statement helped my team switch from focusing on what they didn't want or like to focusing on what they desired. Documenting and committing to their desires brought accountability for developing their personal best in response to the challenges we faced. It also allowed for vents on difficult days. However instead of complaining, they would blow off steam with the intention of shifting into a position of choice and greater personal Power. We became a team working with the changes, offering suggestions and playing the game, knowing that we were developing leadership, self-management and communication skills in the process. In the fifth reorganization, my team was disbanded. Two team members were promoted to managers and the rest took positions on other teams. No one lost their job. I was the only one offered the choice between a three-month severance package or another lending position.

As we used the many restructuring events to reflect on who we were, what we stood for and how we wanted to ride the changes, I named my mission, found some answers to my persistent life questions and the courage to walk away from a paycheck. I didn't even know what I would do next when I made the decision to leave. To bridge my path from banker to mind-body coach, I adopted a variation on the tool successful companies use to guide their efforts: a strategic plan—but with heart. Since the plan was for me, I called it a Me, Inc. strategic plan and gave myself a promotion to CEO of Me, Inc., acknowledging that this was my way of aligning with my Authentic Power and what I would do next. A happy result was that I started and grew my business using less effort than I had been taught to exert.

Calling my Me, Inc. strategic plan a *Me, Inc. Treasure Map* came about as my business and personal life evolved. It has been an integral part of my life enabling me to survive, grow personally and thrive in a variety of economic climates since leaving the bank. I update my map annually and more often during difficult times. It helps me stay connected to my Power and to hold, in Blake's words, "...a firm persuasion" of what I truly desire.

The Me, Inc. Treasure Map - Overview

The *Me, Inc. Treasure Map* includes a section that walks you through identifying or clarifying your *Mission*. It also has sections for developing all other components of a strategic plan—*Core Values, Vision, Goals and Action Steps* as well as a section on *Noticing Results.* Unlike conventional business plans, your *Me, Inc. Treasure Map* also places all components into the context of your greater *Purpose.*

The terms mission, vision and purpose have been used interchangeably by many writers and leaders. Distinguishing between them and acknowledging within the treasure map that everything we do helps us fulfill our life purpose, is my unique contribution. For example, as an individual with my own business, my **mission** is "To empower others to live in their Power" while I describe my **purpose** as "To be genuinely happy and to express my Authentic Self in all that I do." If you are an administrative support person, you may define your **mission** as "To help people be organized, efficient and relaxed" while stating your **purpose** as "To be a peaceful and efficient presence in the lives of others." In both examples, a **vision statement** would describe concrete outcomes that you desire—quality of life, wealth, relationships and work, to name a few.

"...everything we do helps us fulfill our life purpose..."

Me, Inc. Treasure Map

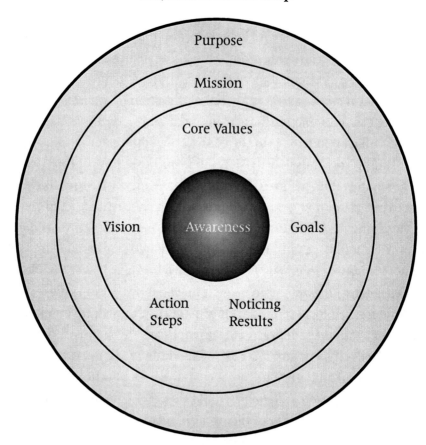

Figure 12.

Figure 12 graphs how your mission, vision, core values, goals and actions steps are all helping you fulfill your life purpose—a treasure that you are discovering and embodying as you live your mission and pursue your dreams. Awareness is at the center because a *Me, Inc. Treasure Map* is a template for consciously living and working.

Your *Me, Inc. Treasure Map* is a tool for proactively directing your journey through crossroads moments. It can also be used for reframing or redesigning *Projection Dilemma* reactions and sub/unconscious beliefs that underpin them, preparing you to circumvent what might take you on twisty, rough-road detours. Here are some examples.

- If you were raised in a family modeled after the traditional father-is-the-breadwinner-mother-runs-the-home structure and you are a woman whose mission calls for her to be a business leader in a local community or a man called to be a stay-at-home father, you may feel conflicted as you fulfill your role. The *Core Values* section of your map lets you clarify your values so they validate your priorities.

- Suppose you learned to hold back your opinion because you were raised in a family that modeled *Children are to be seen and not heard* and, as an adult, you have difficulty speaking up and being direct. Defining your core values so they support safe and honest communications is a way of promising yourself that you will follow through on planned action steps, even if it means having difficult conversations.

If you are at the crossroads moment of starting your own business or making a career move, complete your personal map first and let it direct your efforts. Then use the *Me, Inc. Treasure Map* template for formulating your business plan or focusing your search on companies aligned with your mission, purpose and values. Naming or revisiting "Brand You" at any time reconnects you with the mindset of living from your Power.

Create Your Me, Inc. Treasure Map

As a starting point for developing your *Me, Inc. Treasure Map*, I invite you to playfully begin by giving yourself a promotion to Me, Inc. CEO. You might stand in front of a mirror and read the following certificate aloud to yourself or repeat the words while having a trusted friend read them to you. Substitute your name for "Me," if you prefer. I encourage you to copy and display this certificate where you will see it regularly and celebrate this crossroads moment in your own unique way.

Congratulations!

You have been promoted.
You are now CEO of your own business.
The name of your business is Me, Inc.

Feel free to read the whole book first and return later to design your treasure map. When you are ready to begin, review the *Me, Inc. Treasure Map* components, then pick the section where you would like to start. Some find it easier to define their core values before writing their mission statement. For others, their mission or purpose statements come first. It's your choice. The *Vision, Goals* and *Noticing Results* sections are best done after the *Mission, Purpose* and *Values* sections because the former says how you plan to put the latter into action. Make your *Me, Inc. Treasure Map* detailed or keep it simple. Mapping your intention has power, whichever approach you use.

Before starting or when you find any component difficult, I recommend activating your whole-brain by doing the Figure 11 *Activities that Switch on Your Whole-brain* (pages 73 and 74). It will help you keep a balance of mind and heart as you create your treasure map.

Mission

Your mission statement describes what stirs your passion or brings meaning to the work you do. It is not your title, the role you play or your to-do list. Much bigger, it is an umbrella covering all areas of your life including how you serve in your family, with your friends, on your job and in your community. Put loving your life together with the willingness to discover more ways to sustain this feeling at work and home, and you launch yourself into living your mission.

Here are some real life mission statement examples:

• A mother has a mission "To create, nurture and maintain an environment of growth, challenge and unlimited potential for all those around me."

• A manager has a mission "To build creative and effective teams."

• A salesperson has a mission "To help people realize their dreams."

The mother's mission can be the same at home and at the office. She can nurture the growth of her children or a team of employees. Likewise for the manager and salesperson. They can build teams and help people realize dreams at work, at home or as a volunteer in the community.

*"My mission in life is not merely to survive,
but to thrive; and to do so with some passion,
some compassion, some humor, and some style."*
— Maya Angelou

Reflect On and Write Your Mission Statement

Think about what you do at work, at home, in the community or at school and ask yourself, *What do I enjoy about what I do?* Then write your first thoughts. Do you love to see people relax and let go of worry as you listen deeply? Do you like to solve puzzles and inspire a fun workplace by creating more efficient systems? Do you enjoy being a resource to people in need?

The first time you complete the sentence, "In my work, I enjoy…" it can be a bit intellectual. You might write something like "I like listening to customers and solving their problems." To get to a more heartfelt description, look at what you first wrote and complete the sentence, "What I enjoy about that is…" Again, write your first thoughts. If necessary, do this a couple more times until you capture the passion you get from what you do.

When your words originate from your Authentic Desire, you might write, "I enjoy watching people relax and smile when a problem is resolved." When you translate this into a mission statement, you might write, "My mission is to inspire people to smile, relax and enjoy life."

No matter how dissatisfied you may be, there is something you enjoy, if you are willing to acknowledge it. If the rebel in you says, *Yeah—break times, lunch or when the kids are at school!* go with it and explore what about breaks, lunch or having quiet time to yourself you enjoy. Is it the interactions with people, the solitude or long walks you take? Are you helping people troubleshoot their personal challenges on break? Are you reading, wondering if there is a book in you?

In your journal, record your answers to the following prompts, which are designed to help you uncover your mission statement. Make your mission statement general, like the examples listed in the preceding bullets. No need to deliberate endlessly on it. Your mission statement can evolve over time. It is great to review and update it annually or after a period of significant change.

> *"You are either living your mission, or you are living someone else's. Which shall it be?"*
> – Laurie Beth Jones
>
> ## Mission Statement Reflections
>
> 1. In my work, I enjoy …
>
> 2. At home, I enjoy…
>
> 3. In the community, I enjoy…
>
> 4. At school, I enjoy...
>
> 5. What I enjoy about that is…
>
> 6. What I enjoy about that is…
>
> 7. My mission is to….

Purpose

While your mission statement is a general description of what you enjoy doing, your purpose statement describes how you are *being* as you live your mission. Looking back on the mission statement examples:

- The mom would not be nurturing excellence if she were angry and impatient with a child who is struggling with reading. Her purpose statement might be written as "To be present and patient as I guide others."

- The manager would not be supporting team effectiveness if he were to take a phone call or check email while listening to a team member. His purpose statement could be "To model respect."

- The salesperson would not succeed at helping his clients get what they want if he were overly focused on technical features with people who are more interested in how his product will benefit them. His purpose statement may read "To be in rapport with all I serve."

A strong sense of purpose fosters an optimistic outlook during difficult times. An error, illness, injury or misunderstanding can help you fulfill a purpose written as "To be compassionate and forgiving." Serenity can become the norm when you appreciate how well you embrace and move through challenges and are happy with the person you are becoming as you do.

A Real Life Example

A business owner wanted to distinguish herself from other talented massage therapists. She defined her *mission* as "To nurture health and happiness." She knows helping her clients' mental and emotional states affects their level of tension and ability to relax. To draw out happiness in others calls for her to fulfill her *purpose*— "To bring a happy heart and hands to all." Clients who come in angry, upset or depressed invite her to know her boundaries as well as to be kind and patient. She closes each session by giving the client a card with a special affirmation so when the client reads the card at a future date, he or she reconnects with their happy time on the massage table. It is a signature that effectively puts her in a class of her own.

Reflect On and Write Your Purpose Statement

Many times, words seem limited when you are attempting to capture the essence of a life purpose. Feel free to use whatever works for you to depict your purpose, like pictures, poetry and metaphor. I have changed the words and images that describe my purpose many times over the years in an attempt to capture the feeling of it. Let the following prompts stimulate your own ideas and record them in your journal.

"...the greatest treasure is not what I achieve;
it's who I am becoming."
Jo Anna Shaw

Purpose Statement Reflections

1. Imagine yourself as an ideal Me, Inc. CEO at work and at home. How are you expressing yourself and feeling? What qualities are you exhibiting?

2. What you appreciate is a reflection of your purpose. If the ocean, forest, mountain, garden or any creature were an echo resounding your purpose, what would it be? Pick one element or creature and complete the sentences,

   a. "I am _____ (a butterfly, the ocean, a mountain...)."
   b. "I _____ (Describe your qualities and how you engage life.)"

3. Summarize #1 and #2 above and finish the sentence "My purpose is to _____."

Core Values

Core values are guideposts on the path to living your Me, Inc. CEO ideal. They represent qualities, skills and behaviors that govern how you live life or conduct business—how you engage in conversations, handle conflict, deliver service and instruct others. They can be values you learned from others or you can name your own.

The core values I live by are Self-respect, Balance, Kindness, Communication and Excellence. Self-respect invites me to discover and honor my gifts, go my own way and walk my talk. Balance means giving equal time to doing and being, rest and activity, work and play. Kindness reminds me to be kind to myself as well as others. Communication calls for me to speak my truth from my heart, after listening deeply and understanding another. Excellence drives my commitment to timely customer service, quality sessions, trainings and resources. These qualities, skills and behaviors are what I believe will help me eventually fulfill my purpose.

Core Values and Healthy Self-esteem

People with healthy self-esteem have an aura of confidence, competence and steadiness that makes them easy to trust. They know who they are and what they stand for. If this describes you, this section will let you become more conscious of the core values you live by, if you haven't yet written them down. When you give words to what you do naturally, you acknowledge yourself and your role model status. You are a teacher.

People with low self-esteem give their power to *Projection Dilemma* inner voices or turn it over to others by discounting their own needs or desires. If this describes you, exploring your core values will invite you to reach deeply within yourself for the knowing that you have a right to have and live by your own values.

I use the term healthy to describe self-esteem, instead of the term high, because people perceived as having high self-esteem are not always at their best when voicing their opinion or taking action. When taking risks, being proactive and voicing opinions are for proving oneself or without consideration for their effect on people or systems, these actions are indications of low self-esteem. Core values such as Quality, Sincerity, Consistency and Communication guide development of awareness of how others may be affected by your words or actions.

Some core values that help you to cultivate healthy self-esteem include Trust, Courage and Communication. Trust could be further clarified as trusting yourself, others and life. This intention affirms belief in yourself and the desire to build self-confidence. Courage as a core value can support risk-taking, like asking questions that facilitate decision-making, setting boundaries or reaching out for help. Communication as a core value may be used to ensure accountability for voicing opinions and getting to the point.

A Real Life Example

A client was dissatisfied about the direction her community service group was taking. She was unhappy because she was not speaking up and was judging herself for allowing a direction she had not agreed to. She was in the *Projection Dilemma*, stuffing her feelings, holding back her opinion and uncertain whether to stay or walk away. When she accepted her promotion to Me, Inc. CEO, remaining in the group became secondary to the self-esteem she would gain by living from her Power. She identified her core values of Honesty, Commitment and Service. In a mind-body coaching session, she embodied them. Thereafter, she was able to raise her concerns and reach consensus as she asked the group to refocus.

Reflect On and Define Your Core Values

Notice the values modeled by those you respect. Are they Self-reliant, Efficient, Organized and/or Direct? Are they Family-centered, Compassionate, Deep Listeners and/or Balanced? Notice what annoys you. For example, if interruptions bother you, you value Respect. If poor listening frustrates you, you value Listening. If tardiness triggers you, then you value Timeliness.

The words you choose for core values can mean many things to many people. The power of naming core values comes from pinning down what *you* stand for and what *you* mean by the word you pick. After you name a core value, it is helpful to define it and write an affirmation showing its application. Here are some examples:

- If your purpose is "To be trustworthy and accountable," one of your values may be Excellence—defined as "Doing things right the first time." An example demonstrating its application could be written, "I politely let people know, in advance, my approach to projects and why. Then I confirm agreement with my timelines before beginning."

- If your mission is "To inspire collaboration" and you enjoy brainstorming in an interactive work environment, you may name Teamwork as one of your core values—defined as "Being a collaborative participant that honors the ideas of others." An example demonstrating its application might be written in this way: "I prepare for and actively participate in meetings. I acknowledge the contributions of others before offering my ideas."

- If you admire those who are helpful, you may name a core value of Balance—defined as "Being rested and refreshed when helping others." A demonstration of its application may be written as "I say no to requests for assistance when I am tired."

Let the following *Core Value Word List* and the *Core Value Reflections* which follow guide you as you think about the qualities, skills and behaviors you would like to express when living your mission and purpose.

Core Value Word List

Accountability	Family-Focus	Organization
Accuracy	Fun	Productivity
Action	Generosity	Quality
Awareness	Goodness	Respect
Balance	Happiness	Resilience
Caring	Health	Self-respect
Consistency	Honesty	Self-reliance
Communication	Inspiration	Serenity
Commitment	Integrity	Service
Compassion	Intelligence	Sincerity
Courage	Kindness	Teamwork
Deep Listening	Laughter	Timeliness
Directness	Love	Timelessness
Efficiency	Mindfulness	Trust
Excellence	Non-Violence	Understanding

"I love those who can smile in trouble, who can gather strength from distress, and grow brave by reflection. 'Tis the business of little minds to shrink, but they whose heart is firm, and whose conscience approves their conduct, will pursue their principles unto death."
Leonardo da Vinci

*"Your beliefs become your thoughts. Your thoughts
become your words. Your words become your actions.
Your actions become your habits. Your habits become your values.
Your values become your destiny."*
Mahatma Gandhi

Core Value Reflections

• List the core values you were raised with. Circle the ones you resonate with, put a question mark by those you would redefine and draw a line through the ones you no longer believe in.

• Think about someone (past or present) you admire. What qualities do they have that you appreciate?

• Think about the last time you had a miscommunication with someone. Imagine the conversation going well. What positive qualities are you demonstrating?

• Think about the last time you let a task or event upset you. Imagine dealing with the situation positively. What qualities are you demonstrating?

1. Core Value #1: _____
   a. What do you mean by this?
   b. Write an affirmation that demonstrates how you will apply this core value.

2. Core Value #2: _____
   a. What do you mean by this?
   b. Write an affirmation that demonstrates how you will apply this core value.

3.Core Value #3: _____
   a. What do you mean by this?
   b. Write an affirmation that demonstrates how you will apply
   this core value.

4.Core Value #4: _____
   a. What do you mean by this?
   b. Write an affirmation that demonstrates how you will apply
   this core value.

5.Core Value #5: _____
   a. What do you mean by this?
   b. Write an affirmation that demonstrates how you will apply
   this core value.

Vision

Another step in designing your *Me, Inc. Treasure Map* is creating a
vision board that out-pictures the vision of what your lifestyle,
work, finances, relationships and material possessions would look
like, as a result of living your mission.

The act of imagining, externalizing and displaying your wildest
and most practical desires, especially if you were not allowed to
express them when you were young, can reconnect you with your
Innate Power. Using a playful approach and making it safe to revisit
your youthful dreams with innocent curiosity makes it possible for
you to either find peace with the path you have chosen or see the
clues directing you to honor your original dreams. As you allow your
desires, feel them and consciously choose the ones you will act upon,
you unleash your Innate Potential to be all you dream of being.

A Real Life Application of Using a Vision Board

There was a time my vision board had images of me conducting workshops reaching many more people every year. At the time, I was holding seminars in my living room with twelve or less participants exploring movements that help complete developmental stages and resolve learning challenges. When we entered difficult economic times, that aspect of my work came to a screeching halt, in spite of having imagined it expanding and increasing my outreach efforts.

At that crossroads moment, I chose to explore other ways to conduct workshops, since they are an aspect of my work that I enjoy. This led me to fall back on my experience in the corporate world. I contracted with a national business training firm and stepped into a part-time position conducting one hundred and thirty seminars a year for thousands of people looking for ways to enhance their communication and leadership skills. This direction initially felt like a detour into my past. In hindsight, it awakened my clarity and confidence as well as a renewed motivation for devoting the time and resources it took to write and publish this guide.

When I returned home from trips, occasionally I would walk into the room where I display my vision board and look at it. Seeing and feeling the contrast between the pictures and words on my vision board and the life I was living—with its many stresses— motivated me to take action toward moving on.

With the help of my coaches, I uncovered the clues that were inviting me to upgrade old ways of being and applied many of the activities I present in this guide to my life. After nearly four years of traveling and teaching someone else's curriculum, I rescinded my contract so I could devote myself to redeveloping my local business and writing this guide.

Like a spiral, previous work may come around in another form when we are able to bring new skills and wisdom to it. Revisiting and updating your vision board at crossroads moments is a way to keep your progress in perspective and avoid the *Projection Dilemma*. Instead of getting upset and giving up when things don't go as planned, it becomes easier to optimistically embrace what shows up and do your best. You never go backward when you live with the intention to be and do your best.

"You never go backward when you live with intention to be and do your best."

Reflect On and Map Your Vision

Pick someplace where solitude and nature can open the doorway to connecting with what you would be doing and accomplishing when you are fully living your mission, purpose and values. Bring a pad of paper, journal, writing and drawing tools, old magazines and anything else you would use to capture your thoughts and feelings. Images and words are not as crucial as the feeling and intention you bring to this activity. For best results, be playful so you create your vision board from your Innate, playful Nature.

Enter the following *Vision Reflection* activity after using the *Meditation Protocol* (page 28) to open your mind and heart. Set your intention to unearth the treasure of your deepest desires and allow your imagination to reveal images and words. Be childlike and curious. Let your thoughts and images flow freely and put them on paper without editing.

As you map your vision, reflect on whether it is your Me, Inc. CEO's desire or a dream adopted from someone else. Bless and remove anything

"As you map your vision, reflect on whether it is your Me, Inc. CEO's desire or a dream adopted from someone else."

from your vision board that is not authentically what you desire. Leave those items that bring peace, a quickening or a smile to your face. When you are done, compare your vision to your mission, purpose and values and notice if they are congruent.

"If you can dream it, you can do it..."
– Walt Disney

Vision Reflection

Use the following prompt to get your vision board started.

• In first person, describe the qualities of your ideal career, relationships and any activities that nurture your talents, creativity and love of life. Some statements I wrote while creating my vision board began with "I wisely use my time, talents and treasures to...", "I greet each day with gratitude for my life, work, friends and family...", "I am financially free and make a difference by...", "I celebrate my creativity by gardening and..."

When you are done writing, put your vision on paper as a collage using words or some other artistic rendering. Honor your unique learning style. Use a recorder or three-dimensional materials if you find them more desirable. You can see by my vision board that it doesn't need to be a great work of art.

After Constructing Your Vision Board

Some like to display their vision board where they can see it regularly. Those who are familiar with software programs like PowerPoint and Keynote enjoy building theirs in these formats, together with special music and graphic transitions. I did this once and found it fun. My current vision board is on a wall in a special room where I easily see and update it as my life evolves. At other times, it has gone into a box or a drawer only to be found later. It is enjoyable to find and review a vision board several months or years later and be amazed at how much was accomplished. Pick an approach that fits your style.

When opportunities come along that are not on your vision board, look to see if what shows up fits your mission, purpose, values and goals. Some will, or will appear to, and some won't. For instance, I find it curious how many times I am approached with the latest network marketing business opportunity when I'd like more cash flow. They seem to appear out of nowhere. A few looked so attractive I even signed up. Each brought lessons instead of financial rewards. After a few of these detours, I discovered how crucial it is for me to focus on the core business I love if I am to have my treasure. I have learned that relying on potential monetary outcomes as the primary motivation for undertaking and attempting to run two businesses goes against my values of Self-respect and Balance.

Whenever a crossroads moment or a "once in a lifetime" opportunity comes along, stop and revisit your *Me, Inc. Treasure Map*. As part of your decision-making process, meditate or walk in nature with the intention of having clarity arise from a peaceful connection with your

"There are no wrong decisions when you grow through detours and enjoy the fruits of your efforts."

Power. Feedback will be provided by whatever path you choose. Along the way, you may learn some lessons or discover unexpected treasures. There are no wrong decisions when you grow through detours and enjoy the fruits of your efforts.

Goals and Action Steps

Setting goals and taking action are interim steps that bring your *Me, Inc. Treasure Map* to fruition or give you feedback so you can reevaluate and adjust it. Studying a new business opportunity, getting certified in a particular discipline, networking online or in person, scheduling intervals for writing, practicing your art or meeting with a mentor are some examples of goals and action steps that help you bring about what you desire.

Write your Goals and Action Steps

Information overload is resolved when you put your thoughts on paper. It helps you see options and gain perspective. I like to put mine on a large sheet of drawing paper or a white board, so I can place it in a visible place where it is easily seen and updated.

S.M.A.A.R.T. goals are most effective because they are **S**pecific, **M**easurable, **A**ligned with your purpose, mission and values, **A**ttainable, **R**elevant, have a desired completion **T**arget, and are written in the present tense. Here are some S.M.A.A.R.T. goal examples:

S.M.A.A.R.T. Goals:

- I master my job and achieve a promotion to _____ by _____.
- I have a masters degree in engineering by _____.
- I write and publish my book by _____.

- I sit in with local musicians on weekends beginning
  _____ and feel happy with the caliber of my playing.

S.M.A.A.R.T. Action Steps:

- By _____, I join an association of professionals in my field
  and attend their meetings once a month to network and build
  my skills.
- I develop a list of online universities, respected in the field of
  engineering.
- I write for two hours a night two nights a week and on
  Saturday mornings, and finish my first three chapters by
  _____.
- I practice guitar three nights a week for a minimum of thirty
  minutes.
- I schedule and stick to a daily routine that begins and ends
  with meditation, includes one sit-down meal with my family
  and a half-an-hour walk.

List your goals and identify which ones are basic needs, which are
discretionary and which are essential to living your mission and
realizing the vision you mapped. Basic needs like food, shelter,
clothing and safety come first. Only when your basic needs are met
will you have the peace of mind and where-with-all to focus on
actualizing greater desires.

Generally, eighty percent of your results are achieved by twenty
percent of your efforts. Keep it simple. Answer the following
reflection questions then set your priorities by asking, *What top three
goals or action steps will allow me to move closer to or unearth my treasure?*
and work those first.

Remember to put your action steps on your calendar before
scheduling your responsibilities to others. Persevere until your goals

are reached or changed. If you find everyone else's priorities taking precedence over yours, you may want to meet with a coach or mentor to discuss your concerns and options. If you achieve your goals before the target date, stop and celebrate so you reinforce taking action from your Power.

"I am free to be what I want to be and to do what I want to do."
Jonathan Livingston Seagull
(Richard Bach)

Goal Setting and Action Step Reflections

1. What unmet basic needs do you have, if any? How and when will you address them?

2. What are your top three priorities?
   a. When is the most convenient time for one or some of them?
   b. Schedule them on your calendar.

3. What activities will contribute most to your health, peace and happiness?
   a. When is the most convenient time for them?
   b. Schedule them on your calendar.

4. Look at your vision board.
   a. What are the top three outcomes you desire?
   b. What is one activity that will begin to bring one or some of them to fruition?
   c. Schedule the activity on your calendar.

Notice Results

Noticing results is a crossroads moment. It is helpful to begin with acknowledging and appreciating when you are living your purpose, mission and values. These times are when you are functioning as Me, Inc. CEO.

Me, Inc. CEOs are impartial observers who admit that they may not know everything in advance that can influence their results. Their attention is on looking for what is *different* and positively acknowledging *any* change while detaching from outcomes, knowing this approach is the shortest path to their treasure.

Looking at outcomes through the projector on your head, focusing on what you haven't accomplished or criticizing yourself for unwanted

"Your choice to embrace your results with openness and curiosity enables you to make the best of whatever outcomes unfold."

outcomes will bring you misery, as well as an inability to see the clues that your results are revealing. View your results with innocent perception and you will find yourself exploring what you can learn from them, what adjustments may be called for or what your next steps might be. Remember Clue #12 (page 60): "Out of your use of awareness comes all that you experience." Your choice to embrace your results with openness and curiosity enables you to make the best of whatever outcomes unfold.

Track and Acknowledge Your Progress

I track my progress by journaling. Bringing an attitude of *progress not perfection* is most useful as I notice my growth and results. You may choose to dedicate a journal or calendar for acknowledging your progress or just keep it simple by taking a time out periodically to celebrate the gems you experience along the way.

If you schedule activities that don't get done, ask yourself if you honored your values when you set aside your priorities for other people or activities. If increased self-esteem is desired, acknowledge the steps you take toward your goals, no matter how small or brief. Reschedule or re-evaluate the importance of anything you don't get to. Besides noticing material gains and achievements, appreciate how well you are living by your core values, loving your life and fulfilling your purpose. Let the following *Reflections on Noticing Results* be your guide.

"Give the world the best you have and the best will come back to you."
– Madeline Bridges

Reflections on Noticing Results

1. What is different since you initiated your Me, Inc. Treasure Map or your last review of its components?

2. What will you continue doing?

3. What will you stop doing?

4. What will you start doing?

5. How are you responding to your results?

6. How are you living your mission, purpose and core values in your present circumstances?

7. What are your results showing you about your commitment, priorities or the need for re-evaluating any component of your Me, Inc. Treasure Map?

8. How do you celebrate your progress?

Clue #19: Designing Your Treasure Map is a First Step

Designing your *Me, Inc. Treasure Map* is a pivotal intention-setting step. Your next steps will be guided by it. I have a friend who found renewed appreciation for his career after previewing the idea of having a *Me, Inc. Treasure Map* in an earlier version of my manuscript. He realized that his current position was allowing him to live his mission and values and was able to let go of frustration around not yet having his own business. Going into his own business may still happen at some future time. Alternatively, he may find that he can fulfill his purpose right where he is. His next steps, whatever they may be, will be the most meaningful and successful when motivated from appreciation of, rather than frustration with, his current circumstances. His ah-ha was that he can become the living vessel of his wisdom, love and joy right now, regardless of the direction he chooses—which fulfills his purpose.

Each time I update my *Me, Inc. Treasure Map*, my desire to have all I create and share come from alignment with my Innate Power is top and center because I live in peace and joy when I do. Writing my book, coaching others and balancing my life by nurturing friendships and reconnecting with horses are current activities that I believe will best help me fulfill this purpose. There came a time, while following my map, where writing this book became more important than anything else in my life. If I had to sell my house or get a low-stress job, I was willing. The more I emphasized who I was becoming as I wrote and patiently edited unclear or incongruent parts while doing those activities which kept me balanced, the more I lived from my Power in all areas of my life.

Letting your *Me, Inc. Treasure Map* guide your life is a provocative, sometimes rocky, process of flowing with setbacks and detours as well as appreciating progress. *The Path of Courage* guidepost, coming up next, prepares you for navigating potential resistance that can arise from your Self-editing parts and from important people in your life, as you go for your treasure.

Guidepost 5:
The Path of Courage

Moving

Like sneaking up to watch
a newborn fawn finding its legs
and mother's nipples,
I approach each drawer and closet
carefully feeling, sorting
and questioning each item

keep?   pass on?   toss?

unworn socks, suits and blouses
pass on

speaker cords from original homeowner
pass on

ballpoints that no longer write
cast that set my broken wrist
food dated over 10 years
toss

bottle opener
designed to pop wrinkle-ridged metal tops
memories of Budweiser drinkers
pass on?   toss?   pass on?   toss?
pass on

ex's "Manifesting Series" cassette tape copies
never worked
toss

rolling pin never used
maybe I will learn to bake bread
or is it pies?
keep

umbrella fichus and split-leaf philodendron
long time housemates too large for my new place
pass on

geraniums
still putting on new stalks and flowers after ten years
they can winter over by the kitchen window
in the new home
keep

bridle, snaffle bit, reins
leather still supple
he said, "Take care of your tack and it will last forever."
keep

house clean and empty
I close the door one last time
on a lifetime lived
in twelve years on six acres
drive to the foot of the driveway
get out of my car
face the land
thank the pine, madrone and oak forest
say good-bye

a gentle breeze reminds me
I am with you always

I am settling in now
listening to a distant train whistle and freeway hum
watching parents stroll their children
exploring the fenced yard
deciduous trees and bulbs still dormant

a bit wobbly, like the fawn
new to the world
not yet knowing where the nipple is
mother close and nudging

This way.

*"If you dwell in your essence, you will know you are a child
of a friendly universe that seeks to offer you peace
in the midst of a world in turmoil."*
—James O'Dea

A Hero's Journey

I walked *The Path of Courage* almost daily after I committed to overcoming whatever I needed to overcome and doing whatever it took to bring this guide to fruition. As I wrote and rewrote, I would periodically get stuck in writer's block—thinking too much, words in their secret hiding places—and I would call my coach for help in moving forward. I originated one such call because my goal was to finish this book by the end of summer 2014. My inner talk sounded like, *"Successful" (quotes denote my perception) people in this business have resources for their clients. You are never going to get this done, so you might as well give it up.*

"It's your resistance."

While I listen to this and other comments, I consciously breathe and confirm what I think I hear him say. When our call is complete, I hang up the phone and contemplate this one line out of all his comments. I know there is something I am not willing to look at or feel because my buttons are pushed and I shrink when hear him say the "R" word. It is his way of helping me connect with feelings that I am either out of touch with or unwilling to express. I address my emotions by writing or expressing them privately, go for a walk or take a few days off and begin again, when I can write while peaceful and present.

Designing and living the life you love is, for many, a hero's journey: answering a call to adventure, meeting with adversity, confronting and overcoming difficulties, and returning a wiser person. Your hero's journey begins when you answer the call to start your own business, help a company or serve people in some way. Other quests begin when you say, "I do," conceive a child, lose your health or a loved one, or decide to birth a book—whenever you explore any new direction in your life. Whatever your adventure, the people and events that challenge you are calling for you to rise above adversity and become a wiser, more compassionate person— to walk *The Path of Courage.*

"...the people and events that challenge you are calling for you to rise above adversity and become a wiser, more compassionate person—to walk The Path of Courage.*"*

As soon as you put what you believe in and desire on paper, it can bring up cognitive dissonance, a conflict between what you want and what is. For some, this can fuel motivation for taking action and following through. Others may imagine that the pain of being proactive is greater than feeling powerless and surrendering to the status quo.

You walk *The Path of Courage* when you constructively engage the changes that take place as you allow your *Me, Inc. Treasure Map* to guide your next steps, especially when you hear others reflecting *your* doubts in the concerns they raise. This guidepost helps you positively interact with your inner and outer doubters, who you will come to know as Projection, Inc. CEOs. It addresses your own resistance, highlights how and why resistance arises, inspires courage and introduces more activities that enable you to stay true to yourself and your desires, even when others object.

Clue #20: Inner Resistance is a Crossroads Moment

Steven Pressfield, a novelist, wrote *The War of Art: Break Through the Blocks and Win Your Inner Creative Battles* to confront his own writing block. Every time I feel resistance, I remember his words: "Resistance is the most toxic force on the planet...To yield to Resistance deforms our spirit...it prevents us from achieving the life God intended when he endowed each of us with our own unique genius." Pressfield's words motivate me to be with and listen to my resistant thoughts, feelings and/or senses so I can learn from the situation stimulating them. On *The Path of Courage*, resistance is a learning tool.

Being a master of resistance to change and working with others who struggle with their health, career or relationships, I have noticed that resistance has physical, mental and emotional symptoms, which many attribute to stress. Some of the physical ones are muscle tension, gritting teeth, holding your breath and fatigue. Mental indications can show up as over-analyzing, worrying or guilt-tripping yourself out of action steps. Emotionally, resistance can cause you to contract or shrink from your feelings and from following through on what you desire or seeing another's point of view. The following additional insights are not an exhaustive list of other instances in which resistance is present. Please add your own to the list or refer to Steven Pressfield's quick read for more. If you feel your gut or heart contract as you read about the "R" word, embrace it as a crossroads moment—pause, breathe and use any of the activities you have learned thus far to switch on your whole-brain. When you do, you will be shaving the edge off resistance as you read.

Resistance is fear in disguise. It causes you to forget your new year's resolutions. It is why all great intentions get pushed aside by old routines before the third week of January, as with a friend of mine who loves to help others get organized and optimize their use of technologies. She desired more income and her resolution was to begin blogging. She even took classes to learn how. Then she dropped the idea altogether. Her excuse? "I had so many interests, I couldn't decide what to write about and then I got too busy with other things." Maintaining the status quo is the Projection, Inc. CEO's mission.

Resistance causes you to become really skilled at justifying why your co-worker's, friend's, neighbor's or adult child's problem, which they may or may not be perfectly capable of solving by themselves, is a more important concern of yours than taking the action step you scheduled. The Projection, Inc. CEO loudly and critically discounts your worth in favor of the problems of others.

Resistance shows up as not contributing in meetings rather than confronting reactions that might occur when you offer facts and figures people might not want to hear. It causes you to not ask for a raise because you assume the answer will be "No." Resistance turns up as working at a job you hate just because it pays well, or working late under the pretense of dedication, while not admitting to yourself that you are distancing from relationships at home. Avoiding confrontation is one of the Projection, Inc. CEO's core values.

Resistance lets television, gaming, YouTube, Facebook and addictive behaviors keep you from developing and following through on your *Me, Inc. Treasure Map*. The purpose of this Projection, Inc. CEO strategy is to keep you from your Innate Power.

Physical challenges like headaches, indigestion and muscle pain and mental issues like difficulty focusing or concentrating can be signs of resisting feelings or not expressing them. When you deny your desires, it is like putting a lid on a pressure cooker filled with emotions. Eventually, enough emotional steam builds up and blows the whistle. The Projection, Inc. CEO would have you take the route of pain and suffering rather than have you answer the call of your heart.

When inner resistance shows up, it is a clue that you are on the edge of a different, more courageous response, if you would but stop, breathe and ask, "What do I truly desire here?" or "How is this inviting me to live by my values and fulfill my purpose?" It is an invitation for you to surmount the tension between habits and thoughts that keep you from your Power and the call to venture to the edge of your comfort zone, where you are closest to experiencing your Innate Power.

> "What do I truly desire here?" ... "How is this inviting me to live by my values and fulfill my purpose?"

Clue #21: Courage is a Crossroads Moment

I have also learned a lot about *The Path of Courage* as I mine my Inner Treasure. Along the way, I have found that forcing solutions is not courageous. Neither is attempting to please nor hide how I feel, which are fear-based reactions. Allowing and accepting, being curious, open and walking the edge of a comfort zone is what truly courageous people do. The following insights came at crossroads moments, inviting me or a friend to embody the true nature of courage.

> "...being curious, open and walking the edge of a comfort zone is what truly courageous people do."

Courage is love in disguise—love that is expressed in the face of perceived or real adversity as a desire to help others be and do their best, as detachment, forgiveness, self-love and self-respect. Courage is the ability to set aside the habit of obsessing about people, places and things you cannot control or influence, so you can fully present with the person or project in front of you. Being present and extending love are Me, Inc. CEO values.

Courage gives you permission to say "Yes" to your priorities by saying "No" to interruptions or distractions, so you are happy with the quality and timing of what you produce. Courage lets you be the lone questioning voice on a team, so you value your perspective and clarify the ideas of others. It lets you engage others by listening deeply, acknowledging concerns and asking for agreement or suggestions. Me, Inc. CEOs listen deeply and speak truthfully.

Courage allows an executive to approve an innovative new program never before implemented at another company, because she is committed to empowering her team to achieve their fullest potential. Courage sources the ability to walk away from an income-generating business because it is not aligned with your values. Me, Inc. CEOs take risks.

Courage enables you to acknowledge thoughts like *What you want is impractical or impossible, You could hurt loved ones if you make your plan a priority, There may be too many difficult obstacles to hurdle,* and *Achieving your plan could be more dangerous than the status quo.* Courage moves you through the emotions supporting these points of view, so you know the truth as you go for your treasure. A Me, Inc. CEO knows the difference between *Projection Dilemma* beliefs and thoughts that are aligned with his or her Innate Power.

Courageous people know they create their experiences, so they consciously design and live the life they love. They pay attention to life clues, go in the directions they point and appreciate the mountains, valleys and waters they cross, the thorns they get caught on and flowers they pick along the way to their treasure. Me, Inc. CEOs design treasure maps that address obstacles as well as desires.

> *"It is a courageous step to design and begin to follow your* Me, Inc. Treasure Map.*"*

It is a courageous step to design and begin to follow your *Me, Inc. Treasure Map.* As you journey, you may find yourself going against norms—the sometimes unconscious or unspoken "rules" you, your co-workers and loved ones live by. This can cause others to, directly or indirectly, question your motives and do all they can to convince you that your ideas and plans are insane or selfish. I name these naysayers, as well as your sub/unconscious Self-limiting parts, Projection, Inc. CEOs. These are people and inner voices that lead from the *Projection Dilemma*, transferring their worries and concerns onto you based on their perception, then reacting to what they project. When I get triggered by a Projection, Inc. CEO, this perspective helps me manage my emotions and not receive the Projection, Inc. CEO's questions or doubts as personal affronts.

The following clues further compare the *Projection, Inc. CEO's Strategies* and the *Me, Inc. CEO's Strategies*, so you can readily identify which role you or others are playing and make course corrections as you go. In them, you will also meet an exaggerated persona of the Projection, Inc. CEO called the *Antagonist*, learn ways to deal with one as well as tools and techniques for managing your emotions while in their presence. The same techniques are also useful for conversing with anyone who has valid questions or concerns.

Clue #22: Resistance From Others Is Usually Driven By Misperception

A Projection, Inc. CEO believes that protecting you from potential hazards keeps you safe. The challenge is that what the Projection, Inc. CEO sees through the projector on its head is distorted by the history film loaded in its projector. The deeper truth is Projection Inc. CEOs are the ones who don't feel safe. Remember the Clue #8 insight, "Projection equals perception."

Crossroads moments are the meeting places of Projection, Inc. and Me, Inc. CEOs. Generally, the Projection, Inc. CEO inner voices or people you face won't want you or the system to change. The Me, Inc. CEO inner voices or people you face will challenge you to think through your next steps or invite you to move courageously through your resistance. Each has a unique language that makes them easy to spot. I created Figure 13 to help you know when you are hearing an inner Projection, Inc. or Me, Inc. CEO, facing one or being one.

As you look at the difference between Me, Inc. and Projection, Inc. CEO strategies, ask yourself *Which CEO is functioning from the best use side of the Power spectrum? Which one is misusing Power? Which one is resisting change?* and *Which one is taking responsibility and remaining open?*

You are a Projection, Inc. CEO whenever you find yourself using its strategies to deal with occurrences that trigger discomfort. You re-assume your Me, Inc. CEO role when you become willing to take responsibility for your part in the situation. Where there is willingness, there is the ability to perceive more clearly at crossroads moments.

"Where there is willingness, there is the ability to perceive more clearly at crossroads moments."

When you are met with resistance from others, your role is not to determine or tell them which CEO they are being. You are at the helm of Projection, Inc. when you do. Your task is to notice which CEO *you* are being and to practice your *Me, Inc. CEO Strategies* and *Core Values*. Instead of reacting defensively to others, think, *Thank you for questioning me so I can practice my listening and communication skills, learn how to proficiently set boundaries or see what it is like to stand my ground while being respectful to you.* Then engage or take a time out to manage your emotions and contemplate your options.

On *The Path of Courage,* change is accepted as a constant. Projection, Inc. CEOs perceive it as the source of conflict and magnify their conflicted state by resisting change—an exhausting and not very pleasant way of living and working, in my experience. Me, Inc. CEOs constructively engage change knowing that it releases tension, uncovers solutions, builds relationships and creates new, more meaningful possibilities.

Me, Inc. CEO and Projection, Inc. CEO Strategies

Me, Inc. CEO Strategies	Projection, Inc. CEO Strategies
• Be aware	• Deny
• Accept what is	• Blame
• Be proactive	• Avoid
• Do your best	• Force solutions
• Be patient & kind	• Judge
• Focus on facts not opinions	• Withhold
• Set & communicate priorities	• Resent
• Apologize if Projection, Inc. CEO behavior was active in dealing with someone	• Project feelings on others
• Make no assumptions – except that the other person is right from their point of view and be genuinely curious about their perspective	• Be frustrated
	• Make assumptions
	• Make no apologies – say, "It's who I am; get used to it."
• Say what you mean, mean what you say, don't say it mean	• Be sarcastic
• Adapt to personalities	• Demand
• Use active & empathic listening	• Resist
• Don't take things personally	• Expect others to adapt
• Trust	• Control
	• Ignore boundaries
	• Don't listen
	• Interrupt
	• Take things personally
	• Don't trust

Figure 13.

Clue #23: Antagonists Operate Out of Fear and Are Not Rational

Occasionally, you will run into people whose "home office" is Projection, Inc. I call them *Antagonists*. The *Antagonist* has no intention or desire to see you find your treasure, even if they say they do. No matter how positive your intention or proficient you are at communicating and listening, the *Antagonist* persists in being uncooperative or adversarial. You begin to diffuse the *Antagonist's* strategies by understanding their ultimate mission and not taking their comments or behaviors personally.

The *Antagonist's* mission is to survive at all costs. To ensure its survival, the *Antagonist* believes that his or her perspective is the truth, that it is always the other person who has the problem. *Antagonists* also blame problems on events. The economy, the schedule change and the weather offer daily ammunition for negative behavior. For the *Antagonist,* being right, making a scene and locking on to a self-serving agenda take priority over happy outcomes.

Imagine a customer who uses a loud voice and threatening words to get a refund or a discount. The *Antagonist* thinks that trying to upset people by forcing their agenda will get them what they want. When met with impatience, the *Antagonist* is given ammunition to escalate his or her negative behavior. The *Antagonist's* target can even get blamed for his or her emotional state. Even if you remain calm and solve the *Antagonist's* problem, the *Antagonist* might abruptly leave when the transaction is complete.

Antagonists can also be passive in their approach, like those who say they are in support of your dream but continually question or find fault with you or your priorities. More than the fee waiver or the promise of support, it seems the *Antagonist's* true agenda is to ruin your day or to keep you from realizing your dream. Both are true. The *Antagonist* may not be aware of this deeper motivation and the downward spiral it can cause, which looks like this:

1. The *Antagonist* acts.
2. Others react.
3. The reaction or response validates the Antagonist's belief that he or she is right.
4. Problems get inflated.
5. Points of view get inflated.
6. Conflict grows, undermining best intentions.
7. If both parties in a conflict assume the *Antagonist* position, each gets to be right: the other person is the problem.
8. Being right takes priority over following through on best intentions and being happy.
9. Problems and conflicts go unresolved.
10. Positive results get undermined by the need to be right.

You act.
They react.
Your belief about them is reinforced as true.
You get to be right.

You just bought stock in Projection, Inc.

Figure 14.

Antagonists are driven by their middle and back brain survival programs. Their neural networks are not firing sufficiently in their left and right brain to enable them to listen and consider options. As a result, they are not able to be rational so it is not advisable to attempt to reason with them, especially while they are upset. Better to make safety the priority over answering their concerns or demands. Even if they are disrespectful, being respectful as you offer options is how to engage an *Antagonist*.

The Figure 15 activities on the opposite page are designed to help you manage your emotions and respond to *Antagonists* from the best use of your Power. They enable you to remain calm, think clearly and bring the interaction to a close while minimizing the potential for the *Antagonist's* behavior to escalate. Occasionally, emotional outbursts escalate even if you remain calm and do all these steps proficiently. Prepare for this possibility by prearranging permission to hang up the phone on abusive callers or have a back-up person who can intervene or call the police if you have concern for the safety of yourself or others.

When the crossroads moment of meeting an *Antagonist* has passed, allowing time and space (several hours, days or more) before exploring the situation further is a best use of your Power. If an *Antagonist* is a fellow employee, ask your human resource professional for assistance or consider your options for moving on. If you have an *Antagonist* at home, enlisting support from a professional or calling 911 in an emergency is a best use of your Power.

Engaging Projection, Inc. CEOs or *Antagonists* invites us to surmount our own fear, so our actions arise from alignment with our Innate Power. On the Aikido mat, I found that when I was afraid of my practice partner, I wasn't able to remember the technique or was slow in responding. As I studied these reactions over time, I noticed that in the moment of an attack, my breathing was shallow, my heart rate increased and my visual focus narrowed,

Engaging the Antagonist

1. Breathe slowly and deeply.
2. Look at the person's forehead (not at their eyes—a technique martial artists use to stay centered).
3. Remain calm. (Placing your tongue on the roof of your mouth while listening will help slow your heart rate, let you breathe deeper and keep you from speaking prematurely.)
4. Let them vent. (If your hands are free, touch the finger tips of your right hand to your left. It will help you focus. Think, *What do I truly want here? How is this inviting me to live by my values and fulfill my purpose? What does this person truly need?*)
5. When an Antagonist is done speaking, use an empathic statement like "I see this upsets you" or "I hear your concerns." (Or excuse yourself. Water and restroom breaks are great ways to distance from a difficult situation. If you do the Figure 11 *Activities that Switch on Your Whole-brain* on pages 73 and 74, you will return to the situation more in your Power.)
6. State your desire to create a win/win.
7. Ask them how they would like to resolve the situation.
8. If they offer one, summarize how you understand their solution. If they don't offer one, summarize what you understand their position to be.
9. Ask them to confirm your understanding—"Do I understand you correctly?"
10. Close the interaction by saying something like, "I will consider what you have said and get back to you." Specify a timeframe that works for you and then walk away or hang up the phone.

Figure 15.

so all I could see was their fist or weapon. I responded most effectively to an attack when I was able to hold the point of view that the attacker is acting out of fear and I am safe when I breathe deeply, slowly and relax. When I did this well, I could see the attacker's whole body, which telegraphed arm and hand movements before they emerged, and I could respond effectively with the best technique for diffusing the attack. Whenever you feel afraid while in a dialogue with someone, a little movement—place tongue to roof of mouth, breathe deeply, put finger tips together or walk with the person to a table and sit down—can help you calm down and think clearly.

Clue 24: Antagonists and Projection, Inc. CEOs Live by the "Rules" of Their History

The Figure 15 activities are also useful self-management tools that can be applied with anyone who expresses concerns about you or your priorities. In addition to using the Figure 15 activities, self-management is made easier when you remember the Projection, Inc. CEOs and *Antagonists* unknowingly are living by the "rules" of their history. If you are unable to focus, listen and speak effectively under stress, you too are living by the "rules" of your history. At these times, remember another Clue #8 (page 47) insight— behaviors of others are not caused by you. You will not be so easily drawn into another's drama and will more comfortably hold them accountable when you manage your emotions, in the moment, while silently acknowledging the history driving their resistance.

Hopefully, it is a rare crossroads moment when an *Antagonist* shows up in your life. More typically, we all go in and out of our Me, Inc./Projection Inc. CEO roles as we move through the *Four Stages of Self-Awareness*. Mindfulness, balance and positive language, as introduced in Guidepost 2, can prevent lapses into resistance.

Clue 25 shows you how to shift
from resistance to courage when
you become aware of its presence.

Clue #25: Five Steps Shift Resistance to Courage

Accessing courage to engage outer
or move through inner resistance is
a five-step process. First, take a
break to gather your thoughts and
manage your emotions. While on
break, use movement to switch on
your rational brain centers—walk
in nature, write about the situation
or do some activities from Figure

Five Steps to Shift Resistance to Courage

1. Take a break

2. Use movement to switch on your whole-brain

3. Review your Me, Inc. Treasure Map

4. Acknowledge progress

5. Let the next steps arise from your Innate Power

Figure 16.

11, pages 73 and 74. Before deciding how to proceed, take plenty
of time to review your *Me, Inc. Treasure Map* and remind yourself
of your priorities. While you do, acknowledge the ways you are
living your mission and core values, even in the midst of
challenges. Finally, allow your motivation to be inspired by your
connection with your Innate Power and your next steps to be
revealed one moment, one movement at a time. To do this
requires that you let go of your

*"When you truly detach
from an outcome, your next steps
will be revealed and unfold
naturally."*

agenda—be happy whether it
goes your way or not. Writing
this guide flowed when I trusted
these steps. So, too, with insights about your next steps. When
you truly detach from an outcome, your next steps will be
revealed and unfold naturally.

Shifting from resistance to courage is a process of noticing and
embracing the symptoms of resistance and making the choice to

align with the natural flow that happens when engaging life situations and people from your Innate Power. Using *Five Steps to Shift Resistance to Courage* facilitates this. By way of example, many times following my 2001 crossroads moments, I was challenged to trust my choices and these steps. Whether or not I struggled to sustain my trust while doing these steps, my next steps unfolded naturally: receiving help with my recovery, clients showing up when least expected, financial resources materializing so I could continue to live in my home and more. The final two years in my home gave me even more opportunities to practice courage and trust.

This period of time began in early 2012, when I went against my risk-averse, banker program and rescinded my teaching contract—not knowing how the income would be replaced—picked up my manuscript and focused my time, energy and resources on it, thinking I could complete it within a year. Soon thereafter, a synchronous meeting led to a year-and-a-half local training and consulting project, which replaced a large portion of the income I thought I had lost.

By November 2014, my book was in yet another edit process and the stress of being able to sustain funding my house was mounting. One morning, a close friend called asking if I knew of anyplace she could live. I said, "My place, if you would like…" Before her call, I had been resistant to sharing my home. This time I decided to surrender, take my house off the market and help my friend move in. Within two weeks of this, I got a call from my realtor. "There's this woman who looked at your home back in June. She's wondering if you'd be willing to let her see it again." After conferring with my new housemate I said, "Yes, and only if she is a serious buyer and I get my full price." Within forty-five days, we closed escrow, a friend introduced me to a friend of hers who was considering renting her home and, a bit wobbly, I moved not far from where I'd been living.

Clue 26: You Mine Your Treasure On the Path of Courage

Why choose *The Path of Courage*? For me, it is the only path to choose if we want to live in our Power and fulfill our purpose in life. The sign marked "Fear This Way" points to a treasure chest of personal gifts, our ability to share them and an Innate Knowing that holds our next steps. When we learn how to embrace the fear and use the activities given to resolve or walk through it, we get to enjoy mining our treasure in the process. Navigating *The Path of Courage* as you live what you design on your *Me, Inc. Treasure Map* is supported by the skills and tools in *Your Communication Toolkit*, coming up next.

Guidepost 6:
Your Communication Toolkit

Footsteps of Giants

I walk in the footsteps of giants

sharing their wisdom
knowing it belongs to no one.

Some greet it openly
inspired with ah-ha's
take action with conviction.

Some throw up walls
defending old ways.

I invite life-long learning.
Yeses and *Nos* invite me to my own.

I let go,
become the wisdom.

It's no accident we show up in the same room.

"Experience is a wonderful thing.
It helps us recognize our mistakes when we make them again."
—John Contreras

Would Better Communication or Listening Facilitate Your Next Steps?

*Y*ou begin mining your treasure as well as solutions to your crossroads moments by aligning your *Me, Inc. Treasure Map* with your innate desires. You dig closer to your treasure as you engage ever-changing events, make decisions and interact with those who attempt to help or hinder you. Your treasure becomes visible when, even in the most difficult conversations, you enjoy an increasing frequency of meaningful and productive exchanges.

> *"Your treasure becomes visible when, even in the most difficult conversations, you enjoy an increasing frequency of meaningful and productive exchanges."*

Our words, body language, tone of voice, pace of delivery, how we organize and deliver our content or ask questions all influence the outcomes we create—body language and actions contributing most. Emails and text messages are quick ways to schedule, confirm appointments and stay in touch. They have their limitations because words can be interpreted in many ways without the benefit of hearing the other person's tone of voice or seeing their body language. Online, there are many studies demonstrating that between eighty and ninety-five percent of communication is non-verbal. No matter how reliant we become on our technologies, they will never replace face-to-face meetings when asking for support of your *Me, Inc. Treasure Map,* sharing concepts, nurturing intimacy or resolving conflicts. *Your Communication Toolkit* emphasizes healthy in-person communication skills, for this reason.

As you enter this guidepost, reflect on the situation that led you to pick up this guide. Ask yourself if clearer communication or listening might resolve a conflict in your present crossroads moment or unearth your next steps. If you think they could, I recommend writing about and rehearsing what you would like to say using the tips and tools in *Your Communication Toolkit.* If after voicing your ideas and listening to the response, you are ready to go a new way, these tools will help you close doors, bridge transitions and open new doors. They can also help you salvage and deepen relationships as you go.

Tool #1: Verbal Aikido

More scary than falling and tumbling, the most difficult movement I practiced in Aikido was *irimi (pronounced ee-ree-mee),* which means to enter. Being a master of running away, blending in and hiding made it very difficult for me to assertively take on an attacker. The Aikido training mat became a safe place for me to gain and attempt to master self-awareness and self-confidence, while being mindful of an assailant's timing, my surroundings and possible actions. Eventually, practicing Aikido made alternative *irimi* actions available to me when needed. It also helped me value my preferred movement strategy called *nage (pronounce nah-gay)*, which means blending with and falling away from harm, as I explored which one was the most appropriate response in any given moment.

Your life is an Aikido mat. Assertively asking for support,   *Your life is an Aikido mat.* speaking up with ideas or suggestions and other confrontation-like communication strategies are how you practice *irimi.* Listening deeply, easing into a conversation and clarifying with open-ended questions or not acknowledging and choosing to walk away are how you practice *nage.*

You practice verbal Aikido when you are present, listening deeply and using assertive communication skills, while seeking to have a positive exchange. If someone throws a verbal punch, you as a verbal aikidoist tactfully get out of the way and take the attackers point of view by adapting to their communication style and listening deeply. You are able to move a person physically, mentally or emotionally because your approach creates a safe space for common interests to be identified and win/win solutions explored.

As a verbal aikidoist, you are aware that how you think determines how your body language and tone of voice align with your words and actions, which affects your outcomes. The words you choose are born of your *Me, Inc. Treasure Map* mission, purpose and core values and are congruent with your tone of voice, facial expression and body language. When you are practicing verbal aikido, you are expressing your Innate Power.

Tool #2: Deep Listening

When you realize that the *Projection Dilemma* leads to infinite meanings and interpretations, seeking to understand becomes the primary objective of every exchange. Listening deeply helps you to gracefully circumnavigate difficult interpersonal terrain.

When you listen deeply, you set aside your opinions, stereotypes and assumptions and truly seek to understand another's point of view. You listen to sentences and facts as well as the meaning behind what is said. Whether you are certain or uncertain you have correctly understood someone's meaning and content, you confirm or clarify your understanding and ask for acknowledgment so you know the person feels heard and understood. You only explore next steps when there is understanding and agreement to proceed.

When you listen deeply, you turn off your phone or computer screen. You let a speaker know you are following their train of thought by nodding and using vocal acknowledgments. You let them finish a story or their comments before asking questions or initiating problem-solving. If you don't have time to give your undivided attention, you interrupt and schedule a time when you can.

When you listen deeply, you make eye contact without staring, while maintaining a comfortable distance and open body language. Along with hearing a speaker's words and tone of voice, when you listen deeply you notice congruence or incongruence between words, tone of voice, facial expressions and body language as well as your own gut reaction.

When you listen deeply, you take responsibility for clarifying what you think someone has said. If you don't understand something, you might say, "Excuse me; I don't understand your last comment...", "With apologies, I am not sure I understood you correctly. Did I hear you say...?" or "I feel misunderstood; let's begin again."

When you listen deeply, you only interrupt in an emergency. You know that trying to interrupt someone so you can have your say or talking louder while someone else is talking does not create collaboration. Interrupting when someone needs to be alerted to a crisis that requires immediate attention is the best use of this strategy.

There are two listening techniques that, together with self-awareness, facilitate deep listening: active and empathic, also known as compassionate listening. Active listening is when you repeat back exactly what you have heard, as you would when given a phone number. This works best when accuracy is essential or when someone has an accent that is difficult to understand. Empathic or compassionate listening is when you put what someone says into your own words—in one sentence or a few bullet points—preceded by a natural transition like "Let me see if I got this right..." or "Sounds like..." You could also raise a question. If someone makes a general statement about how unreasonable your idea is, you could ask, "What do you find unreasonable about my idea?"

Listening deeply may seem like it takes too much time. Yet in the long run, it builds trust and co-creativity, which expedites projects and conversations. Deep listening draws out the best in you and others, revealing your treasure as you follow your *Me, Inc. Treasure Map*.

Tool #3: Adapting to the Communication Styles of Others

As a verbal aikidoist, you are a deep listener whose ongoing practice is adapting to the communication style of others and interacting assertively. The Tool #4 chart on the next two pages summarizes four main communication styles, including guidelines for understanding and adapting to each. No one embodies just one style: There are an infinite number of unique blends. Yet everyone has a dominant style, which they usually display under stress. The bottom row of the chart invites you to make a note about when you exhibit each style and which one is most dominant when you are under stress.

Tools like this have been used for decades. Applied effectively, they enable you to enhance relationships. The added benefit of mastering the skill of adapting to others is that you develop the other styles. People who are exclusively dominant in one style limit their potential because they are unable to access the viewpoint and wisdom of the other styles. Listening deeply and adapting builds trust when expressed genuinely, while appreciating and being curious about another's unique point of view. These tools can generate conflict if used to control or while seeing people as a means to an end.

Generally, you put this information into action by matching the communication style of the person with whom you are speaking. If they are direct and to the point, you are direct and to the point. If they are focused on details, you emphasize the details. If they are excited, you are similarly animated in your own way. If they are conversational, you relate to them before jumping to the business at hand. You sit if they sit, stand if they stand, look where they look and move in a comparable way. The most natural exchanges occur when you adapt as you would when you greet a baby, genuinely happy to connect with someone.

Tool #4: General Characteristics of Four Main Communication Styles

	Direct	Dramatic	Detailed	Considerate
How to identify	They get to the point and want immediate results	They speak quickly, elaborately and emotionally	They focus on the details, are methodical and precise	They are soft-spoken, polite and friendly
What they want	Results	Inspiration	Accuracy	Connection
What satisfies them	Getting things done	Being appreciated	Getting things done right	Building relationships
When they are upset	They aggressively drive for results	They become loud and argumentative	They ask lots of questions, sometimes more than once	They become silent or withdraw
What they dislike	Wasting time with long stories and too many details	Being interrupted, focusing on details and being too serious	Errors, uncertainty and not enough time to think	Loud, fast, impolite talking, frustration with their questions

	Direct	Dramatic	Detailed	Considerate
Resolve their concerns by	Listening without interruption, being direct, accepting responsibility (if appropriate) and solving the problem	Listening without interruption, acknowledging and appreciating their concerns by paraphrasing and reflecting before solving the problem	Listening, taking notes, confirming understanding in words or in writing, describing the process for resolving the problem, keeping them posted each step of the way	Being friendly and genuinely concerned throughout the resolution process, listening without interruption, advising of the resolution process, thanking them for bringing up the issue
Adapt to their style by	Giving the big picture and using bullet points	Matching their interest and excitement	Showing them the step-by-step process	Matching their friendliness and curiosity
Use their Tool #5 focus/words	Task/ I see... Let's see...	People/ I get... Let's get...	Task/ I think... The fact is...	People/ I feel... It feels like...
Which is your style? When?				

Figure 17.

Tool #5: Preventing Conflicts

Conflicts can occur among people expressing any of the styles or blends of styles. Conflicts are also influenced by a person being task-focused, people-focused, introverted or extroverted. Figure 18 lays these motivations over the four main communication styles. In it, you will notice that direct and detailed speakers are more task-focused while dramatic and considerate speakers are more people-focused. *Detailed* and *Considerate* styles are typically ascribed to introverts while the *Dramatic* and *Direct* styles are usually evidenced in extroverts. Introverts and extroverts as well as task-focused and people-focused communicators have very complementary skills; however, their differing approaches can sometimes cause friction, especially when under stress.

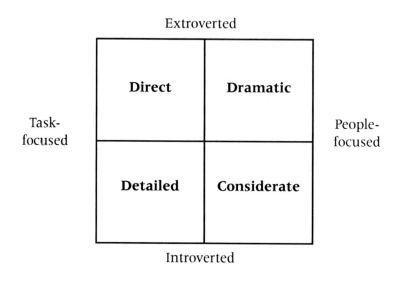

Figure 18.

Conflicts seem to more easily arise between the people with dominant styles diagonally opposite each other. The examples that follow demonstrate how to have smooth communications across the diagonals on the chart. If you sense that your loved one, boss or child has a style diagonally opposite yours, think seriously about adapting before engaging in any "hot" topics. If you notice that a person's style can differ based on the situation and you are not sure how to approach someone, instead of trying to figure out the other person so you can communicate effectively, be yourself and relate in your own style. If the person withdraws, resists or gets upset, their reaction will give you a hint as to their style, the extroverts becoming more animated and expressive and the introverts becoming more withdrawn and soft-spoken, if they say anything at all. Adapt to their response using *Tool #6: Assertive Communication Skills*. If necessary, take a time out and review *Tool #4: General Characteristics of Four Main Communication Styles*.

If your dominant style is *Direct* and you don't adapt well to a person with a *Considerate* style, your approach can trigger a freeze response, causing them to hold back questions or comments that you might want to consider. Allowing a few seconds for a kind, "Hello. How is it going? What are your priorities?" before telling a *Considerate* spouse, child or employee about your plans lets them feel appreciated and gives them a moment to prepare for hearing your ideas.

If your dominant style is *Considerate* and you have a boss, partner or spouse who is *Direct*, get to the point when offering ideas, asking for help or sharing your plans. For example, instead of going into an emotional story and all the reasons you want to do something, give a tweet-length summary of the situation and your suggested solution.

If your dominant style is *Detailed* and you interact often with someone who, in a truly *Dramatic* style, gets really excited about their ideas, your discussion will go more smoothly if you become slightly more animated as you listen and then appreciate their excitement before asking how they are going to fund their proposal.

If you are the one who usually gets *Dramatic* when you are inspired by a new idea, tone your emotions down if you are talking to a *Detailed* or *Direct* style communicator and be sure to include factual support for your ideas.

Tool #6: Assertive Communication Skills

Deep listening, adapting, using "I" statements, clarifying with open-ended questions and stating facts versus opinions are all assertive communication skills. Figure 19 compares how they lie at the center between the passive and aggressive manipulation strategies of Projection, Inc. CEOs. *Antagonists* usually assume fixed positions at the furthest extremes.

	Assertive	
Passive		Aggressive

Projection, Inc. CEO Passive Strategies	Me, Inc. CEO Assertive Strategies	Projection, Inc. CEO Aggressive Strategies
• Listens selectively • Uses "They" statements when blaming • Hints, implies or alludes to, so as not to draw attention to what they really think or mean • Tone of voice is whiny, flat and soft • Says "Yes" even if they mean *No* • Says one thing, does another • Uses small body language • Avoids eye contact	• Listens deeply • Uses "I" statements • Uses "You" statements only when giving a compliment like "You are such a joy to be or work with." • Tone of voice is varied depending on the person and situation • Says "Yes" with explanation • Says "No" after acknowledging and understanding • Uses open body language adapted to the person and situation • Makes eye contact showing interest	• Listens selectively • Uses "You are" statements when blaming • Uses "You need to" statements when telling what to do • Tone of voice is loud, varied and abrupt • Says "No" without acknowledgment or discussion • Says "Yes" without explanation • Uses big body language • Stares

Figure 19.

"I" Statements

"I" statements acknowledge that everything you say is based only on your perception. "I" statements are most successful when you adapt them to the communication style of the other person. Task-focused people will say things like "I think..." or "The way I see it is..." People-focused people will talk about their feelings and senses. They say things like, "I feel..." and "My sense is..." An empathic acknowledgment adapted to a task-focused person would sound like "I see your perspective..." or "That thought makes sense." One adapted to a people-focused person would sound like "I would feel that way, too..." A direct statement can substitute for an "I" statement. Direct statements like "Let's start again", "Let's meet at the coffee shop and talk about this later", "Let me have your name and number" or a simple "Yes" or "No" to questions calling for a yes or no answer are some examples.

Sometimes the statement "I understand..." can backfire. If you haven't demonstrated your understanding by paraphrasing what you heard, the other person may or may not speak the offended inner voice that is screaming *No you don't!* To prevent this occurrence, instead of "I understand...", empathetically name what you understand by saying, "I would be frustrated too..." or "It can be confusing." The other "I" statement that can backfire is "I'm sorry." Used too often it makes you feel like a sad and sorry person. In an organizational setting, apologies are necessary. Instead of saying, "I'm sorry..." for a computer error that was not your fault, use a business apology like "I apologize for the inconvenience or error..." If you are a person who easily empathizes with others and you field lots of complaints, empathic statements and business-like apologies will help you stay nicely detached and keep you from taking on the emotions of others.

Open-Ended Questions

Open-ended questions begin with How and What. They help you achieve understanding. Questions beginning with When, Where and Who clarify specific details and are best used when you need to gather information so you can properly guide someone or when your job is to interrogate.

How and What questions generally work better than Why questions because the Why question is one that can trigger the *Projection Dilemma*, unless delivered with empathy. Remember how you reacted to your four-year-old who asked the Why question one too many times? Remember how it was as a teenager when your parents drilled you, with big judgmental voices, "WHY did you do THAT?" Why questions can cause the receiver to don their movie projector and become CEO of Projection, Inc. Unless you can ask, "Why...?" with heartfelt compassion, you might consider dropping the use of Why and ask How or What questions in its place.

"How did you arrive at that conclusion?" or "What leads you to think my ideas won't work?", delivered with genuine curiosity, will uncover a person's thought process instead of resistance. If they say, "I don't know...", give them time to think about it. Teens and introverts need time to think before they answer and will often say, "I don't know" instead of, "I need time to think about that." Saying, "If you did know, what do you think it would be?", followed by a long pause, can sometimes get a response when a person reacts by shutting down.

Facts Versus Opinions

Unless it is a compliment like "You are such a pleasure to work with...", "You've made my day..." or a statement of fact like "You may be right" or "You're right", a sentence beginning with "You..." usually follows with an opinion, precedes blaming or can come off as being too directive. Direct and "I" statements are most effective when they are based on facts. Here are some ways opinions are expressed and suggestions for using facts instead.

Opinions	Facts
1. "You always interrupt me..." or "You never listen..."	1. "The last time we talked, I didn't feel heard..."
2. "You are so _____ (kind, generous, lazy...)."	2. "When I see you _____, I think you are so _____."
3. "_____ is such a procrastinator."	3. "It is late and the report is due first thing tomorrow. I wonder if ..."
4. "You are so irresponsible..."	4. "I am disappointed that you didn't arrive on time."

Figure 20.

Non-verbal Communication

EYE CONTACT

In our western society, people make judgements about our confidence and truthfulness by how we make eye contact. Healthy eye contact is looking someone in the eye, without staring. If this is difficult, look at the bridge of a person's nose. They won't know the difference. With appropriate eye contact, your eyes will blink naturally every three seconds or so. If you notice that you are staring at someone, blink. If you need to look away for a moment to gather your thoughts, that is natural. Some people need to look up, down or to one side to remember something or to think about what to say.

In a Tibetan tradition, the left eye is considered the window to a person's soul. I've heard it said that if you want to speak to someone on a heart level, focus on their left eye as you talk. If you want to meet them on an intellectual level, focus on their right eye. In my experience, it makes a difference. See how it works for you.

TONE OF VOICE

A gentle smile and breathing deeply as you speak supports a confident and compassionate tone. A serious look can generate a direct and definite tone. When you get excited, your pacing increases and tone rises, reflecting your enthusiasm. When you are concerned or hear sad news, your pacing should slow down and your tone lower as you acknowledge the news.

PHYSICAL STANCE, SITTING POSITION AND FACIAL EXPRESSIONS

Some women fall into the habit of standing with weight mostly on one leg, which causes their hips to be uneven. Standing with weight evenly distributed on each foot, hands at your sides or holding a note pad exudes interest and confidence. Some men have the habit of jingling change or keys in their pockets while standing and talking, which is distracting and an indication of nervousness. I have seen both men and women talking while their arms are crossed. Crossing your arms is okay if you are consciously mirroring another to build rapport. If you do, cross them loosely and you won't appear to be closed. Otherwise, let your hands rest at your sides where they can gesture naturally. Then your body language communicates openness and confidence.

Sitting up straight with finger tips touching and both feet on the floor also communicates openness and trust. If you are too relaxed in your sitting position when listening to someone, you may be perceived as uninterested or arrogant. If your brow is wrinkled when you are listening, people may think you are judging them. Smiling or using a neutral expression is most effective.

Occasionally, I consult a doctor who is a master of listening with his whole body. He sits forward in his chair, finger tips together or ready to take notes on his laptop. He makes eye contact with bright and smiling eyes. His brow is relaxed. He nods. His expression changes to acknowledge my happiness or concerns. His approach helps create a safe and collaborative partnership in healing.

I find the best way to notice body language and facial expressions is to video myself or rehearse in a mirror. When I saw that my nervousness didn't show when I assumed a solid stance while speaking, I was amazed. It was the best confidence boost I ever received in overcoming my public speaking fear.

Clue #27: Your Practice is to Relinquish Struggle and Enjoy the Journey

Aikidoists master moving from their center, which is inside the body two inches below the navel, by repetitively practicing basic moves in a safe environment. With enough practice, their response becomes automatic when needed. As a verbal Aikidoist, you become familiar with your center and develop the neural fields that support the skill of staying poised under stress when you consistently practice meditation and spend regular time in nature. As a verbal Aikidoist, you repetitively practice these communication tips and tools in simple, non-threatening dialogues so you are well-prepared to apply them when you want to persuade others to shift their physical, mental or emotional position.

In Aikido, we love to practice. We even use the word practice as a noun: Aikido is our practice. We view practicing as a process of self-discovery and self-development. Enjoying our practice helps us stay devoted during plateau times when we feel like we are stuck, regressing or not progressing fast enough. We know that the Aikido mat is a metaphor for life. Off the mat, applying Aikido principles in our life is our practice.

Likewise, your life is your Aikido mat and mastering *Assertive Communication Skills* is your practice, especially at crossroads

"... your life is your Aikido mat and mastering Assertive Communication Skills *is your practice, especially at crossroads moments."*

moments. As you embrace crossroads moments for designing and living the life you love, you will have many opportunities to apply the self-management tips from *The Path of Courage* and the communication and listening tools in *Your Communication Toolkit*. As you practice, you will occasionally notice situations in which you continuously struggle. At Groundhog-Day-like crossroads moments, you can either continue reinforcing or trying to control old habits or walk *The Path of Mastery* on which you relinquish the struggle and resolve your *Projection Dilemma.* Guidepost 7 directs your journey on *The Path of Mastery* so you can enjoy being in your Power as you go for your treasure.

Guidepost 7:
The Path of Mastery

Boxes

I was born into a box
called family
raised in a box
called religion
schooled in a box
so I'd fit into a box
called society.

One day
after decades in darkness
I stood in the Light
outside a corporate box
a casualty of poor investments
in little family boxes.

Birds raised in cages
given the opportunity to fly free
often return to their cage
it's familiar
feels safe.

Not your typical bird
I sort through all my boxes
recycling their contents
one inside another
inside another
inside another.

The last box
contains only a seed.

I linger with this seed
timelessly
plant it
watch it grow
and blossom
realize how simple it is
to live free.

"One day you finally knew
what you had to do, and began..."
—Mary Oliver, *"The Journey"*

How to Mine Your Treasure
at Crossroads Moments

*A*t the *Opening* and *Awakening Stages* of my journey, my motivation for walking my personal growth path was to enhance my relationship with a spouse, partner, boss or family member, or find and be successful doing work I loved. I let my self-esteem be determined by an outer-world focus. I crossed the threshold to *The Path of Mastery* when I shifted my focus from my outer to my inner world, measuring my success by my serenity, happiness and ability to appreciate the many aspects of myself, my path, relationships and the world in which we live.

You will uncover many possible solutions to your crossroads moments by designing and allowing your *Me, Inc. Treasure Map* to direct your adventure, and as you consciously engage the people who walk your journey with you or those you meet along the way. As you quest, you, too, may find that your worldly results are but small gems compared to the Inner Treasure you can mine. On *The Path of Mastery*, there will come times when one or more of your outer outcomes consistently fall short of your desire. These crossroads moments will continually show up—in variations on their theme—until you allow your thoughts, feelings, senses and life conditions to reveal clues for resolving the underlying cause of the effects you are experiencing. This guidepost introduces and shows you how to incorporate into your daily life clues and activities that enable you to eventually shift the cause, so your effects more consistently align with your *Me, Inc. Treasure Map.*

Clue #28: The World is a Mirror

I made significant strides into living in my Power when I realized that reacting from the Projection, Inc. CEO mindset presented an opportunity to see what part of me I was denying expression. I made the connection between my discomfort listening to direct communicators and my own discomfort with speaking assertively. I saw how my fear of authority and public speaking was seeded in how my father delivered his early message, "Children are to be seen and not heard." I know now that whenever I have an adverse reaction to any incident that unconsciously reminds me of some unpleasant memory, the occurrence is a **world mirror** showing what is yet unresolved in me. When the effects of my efforts fall short, this **world mirror** holds clues revealing solutions. Thankfully, my world mirror also shows me how much I have grown by reflecting the abundance of love, friendship, health, money and creativity I enjoy.

"Crossroads moments are world mirrors reflecting all the clues you need for resolving the **Projection Dilemma**, *finding the solutions you seek and mining your Inner Treasure."*

Crossroads moments are world mirrors reflecting all the clues you need for resolving the *Projection Dilemma*, finding the solutions you seek and mining your Inner Treasure. These clues become visible when you stop, notice and learn from your difficulties as well as acknowledge your progress. To begin reading the clues, look in your world mirror with the gentle desire to make the connection between your present thinking, way of being and results, and how people respond to you or how you respond to your life's conditions.

For instance, people will mirror passive Projection, Inc. CEO manipulation by resisting you, as your spouse might, when you ask what he or she would like to do for dinner when what you really want is to go out and eat. Teenagers who, consciously or unconsciously, break rules or hide their activities mirror Projection, Inc. CEO parental behavior. People will mirror your doubts by questioning you and your insecurities by challenging you. Acknowledge yourself for noticing when world mirrors reflect your shortcomings. This awareness enables you to make a different choice.

People also mirror your Innate Power qualities. Your associates will be kind to you and others in your presence when you are kind. They will reflect your appreciation and respect, by offering theirs. Your world mirror will also reflect your Inner Treasure when you are looking past behaviors at an Innate Power expressing through others and seeing in them what they may not be able to see in themselves. When you peacefully and proficiently manage and solve the seemingly unmanageable and unsolvable, the picture in the mirror may look chaotic but the reflection will be of you being the happy eye at the center of the storm. Pause and acknowledge your goodness, compassion, clarity and confidence or any of the other qualities of your Innate Power. When you do, you reinforce those qualities and more frequently, extend them in your life.

Crossroads moments are inviting you to learn how to flow with your world mirror reflections. First notice how the situation stimulates your desire to connect with your Innate Power. Before doing or saying something you might later regret, pause for a moment and remember your Me, Inc. CEO mission, purpose and core values. Your next step is to be conscious of your own *Projection*

Dilemma by making the connection between your present and your childhood ways of being that no longer serve you. (Clues #8 on page 47 and #12 on page 60 will help you with this step.) Set your intention to resolve *Projection Dilemma* habits and address present relationship challenges or life conditions from your Power. Then, put your intention into action by walking yourself through *A Nightly Forgiveness/Appreciation Moment*, which you will find in Figure 22.

Flowing with your world mirror is how you walk *The Path of Mastery*. Clue #29 and *A Nightly Forgiveness/Appreciation Moment* are tools that enable you to do this at the end of your day. Clues #30 and #31 guide you through resolving habits that continue to persist regardless of your forgiveness and appreciation moments.

Flowing with Your World Mirror

1. Notice how your response to current circumstances can also stimulate your desire to connect with your Innate Power.

2. Remember your Me, Inc. CEO mission, purpose and values.

3. Notice your *Projection Dilemma* thoughts, feelings, senses and actions.

4. Intend to resolve your *Projection Dilemma* habits as well as the present situation.

5. Walk yourself through *A Nightly Forgiveness/ Appreciation Moment* (Figure 22, page 159).

Figure 21.

Clue #29: Your World Mirror Invites Forgiveness
and Appreciation

Initially, instead of flowing with my world mirror reflections, I mistakenly approached them as if they were hard work, trying to figure out why they were happening and how to fix them. I surrendered to them when I saw how my life fluctuated between the extremes of a raging river and a dry riverbed when dealing with it from a *fix-my-life* or *fix-myself* attitude. However, it flowed like a gentle stream when I viewed what was being reflected back to me with openness and playful curiosity.

When I was locked on fixing something that wasn't working, I was focused on my problems rather than what I truly desired. As a result, I got more of what I didn't want. In another ah-ha moment, I realized that when my serenity and happiness were based on having people or situations be a certain way, my deeper motivation was still outwardly focused on wanting others to change so I could feel okay. My *Me, Inc. Treasure Map* and *A Nightly Forgiveness/ Appreciation Moment* help me live my values, mission and purpose. The more consistently I interrupt negative thoughts and behaviors and use these tools, the more frequently I see my values reflected in my world mirror. I also notice how I am living my mission and purpose, regardless of circumstances.

Consistently checking your world mirror is forgiveness in action. You are open to noticing one day—sometimes one moment at a time— where you still carry guilt, anger, sadness, fear, resentment and judgment. Then, through your own self-help processes or with the guidance of a professional, you reconcile and resolve these feelings, which allows your Innate

"Consistently checking your world mirror is forgiveness in action."

Powers of compassion, peace, unconditional love and playful curiosity to be expressed.

At one of my happy crossroads moments, I was introduced to appreciation as the gateway to seeing my world mirror reflections with clear perception. I started practicing by making a fresh gratitude list every day, appreciating happy as well as difficult moments, while not looking at previous lists. Keeping this routine up for a year made a wonderful difference in how I felt about myself and situations as well as what I manifested in my life. Yet, I still found myself repeating *Projection Dilemma* patterns and wrestling with my inner critic.

On *The Path of Mastery,* I found a couple of gems that enabled me to significantly reduce the power and frequency of falling into the *Projection Dilemma* or hearing my inner critic's voice. They are *A Nightly Forgiveness/Appreciation Moment* and *The Resolution Steps.* These gems are processes that facilitate forgiveness of myself and others. For me, forgiveness is truly appreciating that others have the right to be uniquely themselves and having no need to change them. Along with appreciating life's ups and downs, practicing forgiveness is teaching me to be humble, loving and understanding, while setting boundaries and not accepting disrespectful behavior.

The first gem, *A Nightly Forgiveness/Appreciation Moment,* is a process I use so I can sleep peacefully after a difficult day or learn from and reinforce days when I am in the flow. With it, I set aside time for being with my world mirror reflections while appreciating happy as well as difficult crossroads moments. Please adapt it to your way of entering dreamtime. Whatever approach you choose, your best shift in *Projection Dilemma* thinking and behavior will unfold when you apply these steps while your brain is cycling in alpha or theta. Review Figure 2, *A Meditation Protocol* (page 28), to remember how to create these brain states.

A Nightly Forgiveness/Appreciation Moment

1. In an introspective frame of mind, reflect on and appreciate your day before going to sleep.

2. Appreciate what you did well to reinforce positive ways of being.

3. Whenever you remember an incident that disturbed you, breathe slowly and deeply, and contemplate what your world mirror was reflecting.

4. Prayerfully ask to view your role in the situation free of self-judgment and criticism of others.

5. Affirm that all involved did the best they could at the time. Yawn and rub your TMJ points (an inch in front of your ears where you feel your jaw hinge) until you relax and feel peaceful.

6. With all your senses, imagine the situation as if it had gone well. Then, let it go.

7. Meditate with an inner smile and go to sleep knowing all is well.

Figure 22.

A day or so following *A Nightly Forgiveness/Appreciation Moment,* it is not unusual to run into the person you were thinking about or find yourself in a similar situation. The person's attitude may be happy-to-see-you, apologetic or unchanged. The situation may be easier or more difficult to handle. Remember, your most important feedback is how you respond. Are you being your Best Self? Are you comfortable whether or not they change? Are you amazed at the synchronicity of a similar event? Or do you get a headache, upset stomach or other physical symptoms, coupled with fear, anger or other emotions? At crossroads moments like these, many will find ways to leave relationships or workplaces. Leaving is an appropriate choice if the person or environment is abusive or toxic.

"...sometimes that elusive **Projection** *Dilemma is...keeping you from problem-solving, gaining desired support or building greater self-esteem."* Yet sometimes that elusive *Projection Dilemma* is the culprit, stirring up physical as well as emotional responses to stress and keeping you from problem-solving, gaining desired support or building greater self-esteem.

Clue #30 explores the possibility that your physical or emotional symptoms might be driven by *Projection Dilemma* misperceptions. It helps you find ways to resolve any *Projection Dilemma* influences on your perception, so you don't make premature decisions or find yourself recreating similar dynamics in a future job or relationship. It helps you further explore the causes of your effects by guiding you through how to read the clues your body mirrors about your sub/unconscious thoughts which, as you may remember from Clue #12, affects all you experience.

Clue #30: Your Body is an Aspect of Your World Mirror

Earlier I wrote, "Our body is our Power's communication device." There are seven main and many lesser channels through which our Power expresses. These channels, also known as chakras or energy centers, are extensions of the physical body. I like to call them channels because on *The Path of Mastery*, I know that opening these channels can be like fine-tuning a wireless signal so the connection with our Power is a clear one. Similar to the Projection, Inc. CEO/Me, Inc. CEO metaphor, the channel metaphor is a practical image that speaks the language of our sub/unconscious mind, which more easily relates to and understands metaphor, movement and energy as opposed to intellectual concepts. We function most capably and live our lives most enjoyably when these channels are open, as depicted in the Figure 23 image.

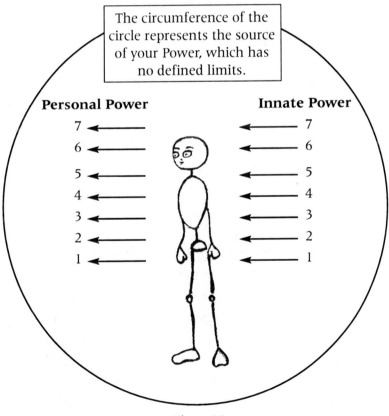

The circumference of the circle represents the source of your Power, which has no defined limits.

Personal Power   **Innate Power**

Figure 23.

*"...we are spiritual beings
having a human experience."*
—Pierre Teilhard de Chardin

Each of the main channels governs different ways we unfold and develop in our life. The first channel, located at the base of our spine, is where our motivation to survive arises. Our desire to birth children and creative projects is rooted in the second channel, at our navel. The third one, in our stomach area, sources our intuition and will power. The fourth, at our heart level, is the origin of our potential to forgive and love unconditionally. Our self-knowledge, self-expression and ability to hear beyond normal hearing ranges arise from the fifth channel, at the level of our throat. The sixth, located at our forehead, enables us to imagine the future and the consequences of our behavior as well as see higher vibrational images and colors, not visible to the physical eye. The seventh channel, at the top of our head, connects us with our higher wisdom and understanding.

The Figure 24 *Opening Your Power's Channels* questions are designed to assist you in identifying and resolving interference so you can make decisions and take action from your Essential Power. Notice, with gentle self-awareness, which channel(s) may have interference. If you have any physical symptoms in the region of a channel, it is not unusual to find your answers to that channel's questions lacking. If you answer any of the *Opening Your Power's Channels* questions *No* or *I don't know,* taking steps to create a *Yes* will enhance your overall well-being.

Opening Your Power's Channels

Channel #1: Are your basic needs for food, shelter, clothing and relationship met? Do you feel safe being yourself—authentically saying and doing what enables you to be happy? Do you eat regularly and sleep well for six to eight hours a night?

Channel #2: Do you express your creativity? Are you honoring your desire to birth children, a business, a book or other artistic endeavor? Do your tools and the people in your life support you in being creative and attaining your desires?

Channel #3: Do you set goals and persist until they are reached or changed? Do you trust your gut? Do you know your boundaries? Do you live by your values? Are you able to allow others the consequences of their behavior? Do you feel content with your work and relationships?

Channel #4: Do you easily give and receive love? Are you comfortable being alone and quiet? Do you appreciate and enjoy your life and the people in it? Do you feel compassion for those less fortunate or struggling? Generally, are you peaceful and happy?

Channel #5: Does your voice project and its tone match your emotional state when you are talking? Do you say what you mean and mean what you say? Are you able to clearly express your thoughts, orally and in writing? Are you able to hear the meaning behind the words people speak? Do you have a kind and encouraging inner voice?

Channel #6: Are you able to focus and concentrate on the task at hand and bring it to completion within required timeframes? Do you accurately estimate the time and effort a task or interaction will take? Can you imagine that you are already living your vision? Do you easily look for and see options? Are you able to identify your mission?

Channel #7: Do you contemplate your greater purpose in life? Do you get ideas for new technologies, processes or solutions to relationship and other life challenges? Do you understand how systems of relationships between people and events affect the whole? Are you able to understand how the details fit into a big picture?

Figure 24.

You begin to adjust the clarity of each channel by affirming the truth of what you believe when your channels are open. Use the prompts in the *Opening Your Power's Channels* to stimulate ideas for "I" statements you can use to guide your steps in opening a channel. Here are some examples:

Channel #1: I am (or feel) safe and at peace. I am in charge of my life. I have all I need to be happy and healthy.

Channel #2: I value and express my creative desires in balance with my other activities.

Channel #3: I trust my gut. I set and follow through on my goals. I feel content and blessed.

Channel #4: I love myself. I gratefully give and receive love. I know what I desire.

Channel #5: I say what I mean and mean what I say. I know who I am.

Channel #6: I see the potential in myself and others. My best is good enough.

Channel #7: I know my purpose. I am a source of creative solutions to complex problems.

Your *Me, Inc. Treasure Map* is also a source of affirmations. You created affirmations when you clarified what you mean by your core values. Your purpose, mission and vision statements can also be formed as affirmations. See if you can identify which channels your *Me, Inc. Treasure Map* affirmations address. If any of the the suggested affirmations or ones you create trigger an inner voice saying, *No you don't*, you have unearthed Clue #31 and an opportunity to apply its *Resolution Steps*.

Clue #31: Affirmations Alone Do Not Open
Your Power's Channels

You cannot overdo the use of positive affirmations when you consider how many years you have been practicing fearful and critical thoughts, and how long you have been allowing television, movie, print and online media to occupy your mind.

"You cannot overdo the use of positive affirmations when you consider how many years you have been practicing fearful and critical thoughts..."

Posting affirmations on mirrors, refrigerators, as screen savers and in other visible locations lets them be subliminal reminders of your desire to live by them. Your subconscious mind is also more open to receiving new beliefs when you repeat affirmations as you enter meditation or while going to sleep and waking up—those times when your brain is cycling in alpha and theta.

Affirmations most effectively assist in opening your Power's channels

"Affirmations most effectively assist in opening your Power's channels when used along with identifying, feeling and resolving one's Projection Dilemma *and reinforcing new beliefs and actions."*

when used along with identifying, feeling and resolving one's *Projection Dilemma* and reinforcing new beliefs and actions. Your world mirror feedback will show resolution or areas where beliefs or skills are still evolving.

If your world mirror isn't aligning with what you affirm over time, instead of becoming a frustrated Projection, Inc. CEO and giving up the use of affirmations, look to the outcome for clues directing you to what is impeding your progress. An affirmation I use is, "I am so happy. My life is so easy. My life is so simple." Occasionally, I get angry while saying it, which is an indication that my third channel has interference—I'm not feeling content and blessed. When I review the *Opening Your Power's Channels* questions, along with not relating to some Channel #3 prompts, I may also find it difficult to answer some of the questions in the first, second or fifth channels. As I address Channels #1 and #2 by balancing work and play and Channel #5 by writing or speaking my truth, I resolve my anger and the interference with my third channel. The more I follow this protocol, the more my affirmation rings true and the more my world mirror reflects ease and simplicity.

Making simple adjustments in your life may be all you need to bring about clarity and the will to follow through on your *Me, Inc. Treasure Map*. The second gem, *The Resolution Steps* in Figure 25, is used for resolving the *Projection Dilemma* habits you find continually reappearing in your world mirror, preventing you from living your Me, Inc. CEO ideals. They are a self-help structure that walks you through looking in your world mirror then applying forgiveness, affirmations, imagination and physical activities to resolve interference with one or more of your Power channels. By going through *The Resolution Steps* when you have some private time after noticing a recurrent pattern, you may eventually resolve the source of what prevents you from knowing your next steps, speaking your truth or answering persistent life questions. You may or may not become aware of what the source was. It may not be possible or helpful to remember. Trusting while doing the activity allows deep shifts. As you do *The Resolution Steps,* remember: your task is not to tear out, remove or destroy unwanted parts of yourself. Your role is to discover what is already whole and beautiful within you.

> *"...remember: your task is not to tear out, remove or destroy unwanted parts of yourself. Your role is to discover what is already whole and beautiful within you."*

If you find any aspect of *The Resolution Steps* difficult to do, seek the support of a trusted professional. Let them know the insights you have gained in using this guide. It will assist you in being a collaborative partner in your healing and personal growth.

The Resolution Steps

1. Notice a recurrent pattern of thoughts, feelings, senses or actions.
   a. Take a time out or do your best, under the circumstances, to bring closure to the event or interaction.
   b. Meditate to reconnect with your Innate Power (Figure 2, page 28).
   c. If you pray, enter *The Resolution Steps* with a request for guidance and assistance.

2. Set your intention.
   a. Write a short sentence that sets your intention to be in your Power, living your mission, purpose and values in relationship to the situation. Be specific. For example, "I am aligned with my Innate Power as I ask for my ideas to be heard."

3. Resolve the Issue.
   a. Write down what happened and how you responded. Write about how the incident was a mirror and the clues it was reflecting about new skills or behaviors you might learn.
   b. Allow whatever feelings may emerge as you review the situation. They can move as part of the resolution process.
      i. If you are sad, cry.
      ii. If you are angry, scream (into a pillow, if you don't want to disturb others) or to blow off steam, do something active like running, playing racquetball or taking a tennis racket to a pillow.

(continued next page)

    iii. If you are afraid, you may feel cold. Wrap yourself in a blanket and yawn.

    iv. If you see humor in the situation, laugh.

  c. Do this breathing technique.

    i. A minimum of seven times, breathe into your lower abdominals (below your belly button) then breathe out slowly. Imagine breathing in your discomfort and breathing out peace, love or joy.

4. Re-pattern your brain.

  a. Do some of the *Activities that Switch on Your Whole-brain* on page 73 and 74. You can use them either during or after Step 3, or both.

  b. When you feel relaxed and peaceful, go on to Step #5.

5. Re-educate.

  a. Go into meditation.

  b. Imagine, with all your senses, the situation or interaction flowing well for you, whether the other person or people seem cooperative or not. Affirm your ability to handle the situation effectively.

  c. When you are done, smile and wiggle your toes and fingers, stretch and have a sip of water. Take a moment to get some fresh air and to be grateful for the blessings in your life.

6. Reflect on the incident that initiated your walk through *The Resolutions Steps* and notice what is different about your thoughts, feelings, senses and experience. Acknowledge your greater perspective. Write down any new insights, ideas or plans.

  a. Revisit your notes after a few days to see if you still feel aligned with them. Note any updates.

7. Periodically use *The Resolution Steps* until you know, in your heart and gut, what you will do next.

Figure 25.

Cultivating an appreciative attitude for all people and experiences in your life as you employ *The Resolution Steps* makes the most of them. Your unconscious mind is literal. It takes what you think and say as fact. If you contemplate *What's wrong with this picture?* or *Why is this not working?*, it will look for all the ways things are wrong or not working. Contemplate instead, *As Me, Inc. CEO, how would I respond?* or *How can I bring my Best Self to this?* Your deeper mind will search for what you can do as well as how you can improve on what you are already doing. Likewise, when you appreciate people and your experiences, your literal brain will look for all the ways they are feeding you.

The *Projection Dilemma's* resolution is allowed, not forced. It happens by the grace of your Innate Power. Your role is to bring a heartfelt intention to have the *Projection Dilemma* resolved, live in your Power, feel your feelings and devote yourself to doing the footwork—meditating, practicing communication, listening and self-management skills as well as getting help, where needed.

Clue #32: Surrendering the Search is a Way of Living on The Path of Mastery

Many clues invited me to go for my treasure as I ventured, unaware of them. I began to notice them more and more as difficult crossroads moments led me to cross from the *Denial*, through *Opening*, to the *Awakening Stage*. On *The Path of Mastery*, I crossed another threshold of understanding as my ability to interpret and take action on my clues increased. Long have I searched for an experience of living from my Power—comfortably speaking from my heart, listening without judgment, easily promoting my business and flowing with people and events, while appreciating my treasure hunt and myself for questing it. On my journey, I have enjoyed many occurrences of being in the flow and those moments inspired me to keep going whenever old patterns would emerge.

One day, a friend of mine suggested that my quest is driven by yet another mistaken perception—that I don't have or am not already experiencing what I seek. I decided to go into meditation to see how I might view this from my Higher Self. Entering meditation, I had the thought *So do I just give up, sit and do nothing?* When I got deeply relaxed, I had the following insight:

That is an option. Sit long enough and you will eventually get up, relieve yourself, eat, sleep and continue with your life. The difference is by surrendering a quest motivated by the perception that who you are, what you have and what you do isn't good enough, allows your living to be an extension of Love in all that you do.

Awakening to living in our Power can be like playing Hide-and-Seek. The search for clues is a part of the game. Sometimes we find what we are looking for. Sometimes we don't so we surrender, tag home and call forth what is hidden. The game of Hide-and-Seek is where we originally learned how to surrender the search. When we design and live the life we love, take our next steps and surrender the outcomes, we become like a spot of ground where nothing is growing—where our Higher Self can germinate, blossom and bring forth that which serves the extension of Love.

> "Surrendering the search is the way of living on The Path of Mastery."

Surrendering the search is the way of living on *The Path of Mastery.* You recognize that who and what you seek is always present and you appreciate the detours you took before coming to this awareness. In his poem "In Baghdad, Dreaming of Cairo: In Cairo, Dreaming of Baghdad," Rumi tells the story of a man living in Baghdad, who dreams of finding riches in Cairo. On waking, he goes on a journey to find the riches prophesied in his dream. By the time he arrives in Baghdad, he must beg for food and money. One night while calling for coins, a night patrolman grabs him and, in his struggle to save himself, he shares his dream. The patrolman is amazed that he had a similar dream but in his, the treasure was in Baghdad, at the exact location of the seeker's home. The lesson?

Yes, the treasure is where you are. Yet without the quest, you may never discover it.

> *"...the treasure is where you are. Yet without the quest, you may never discover it."*

Guidepost 8, our final guidepost, invites you to *Journey in Appreciation*. It shows you how the miracles of appreciation act as a magnet, attracting more for which to be thankful. It provides you with self-reflection protocols that further enhance your ability to *Journey in Appreciation*. Regular self-reflection with appreciation, coupled with designing and living the life you love, enable you to find the gems where you are and see solutions for your crossroads moments. Questing in appreciation allows the causes of your effects to be initiated by your Innate Power, so you enjoy the fruits of your Inner Treasure each step of the way.

Guidepost 8:
Journey in Appreciation

Breathtaking Closeness

> low flying bald eagle
> heading east
> first sighting
> in twelve years of living here

I hang up the phone
after tearful congratulations and appreciations
with my tax accountant
who called to say
how much he valued our once a year
intimate sharing of life challenges and blessings

he tried to say good-bye
as he started to cry

don't run away, I said
I'm not afraid of your feelings

a few more words
promises of big hugs when I arrive
papers in hand
for our last laughter-filled meeting

happy good-byes

> low flying bald eagle
> six foot wingspan
> white crown
> white under-tail feathers
> breathtaking closeness

"Allowance is not a passive acceptance of things as they are, but a recognition that there is something quite beautiful at work."
—Jeshua ben Joseph

The Miracles of Appreciation

I am continually entertained by synchronous events in my life, and they happen frequently because I look for and appreciate them. Rarely do I give time to obsessing about what isn't working. Finding and being with what is working is much more rewarding.

For instance, when I was thinking about how to start this guidepost, a wise friend called after several weeks of no contact. Before saying good-bye, I asked how she is able to appreciate happy as well as tough times in her life, explaining that I wanted to communicate the value of appreciating all life experiences, while honoring how painful and difficult they can sometimes be. "If I had not had the pain of my history, I would not be so focused on being peaceful" was her response. She reminded me how learning to appreciate the events that contributed to my fear of speaking set me on a healing journey that helped me find my voice, *"If I had not had the pain of my history, I would not be so focused on being peaceful."* cultivate healthy relationships and reconnect with my Innate Power.

Appreciation is an act of finding the value, significance or magnitude of people, things and events in your life. It is how you express gratitude. This guidepost invites you to *Journey in Appreciation* by actively looking for the value, significance and magnitude of crossroads and other moments and to enjoy the miracles that happen as you go.

As you *Journey in Appreciation*, you will often be met with seemingly miraculous interactions and events. As if right on cue, when I began the first review and edit of this guidepost, my tax accountant called to say he was retiring and thanked me for ten years of business. On hanging up the phone, a bald eagle flew by my window. After jumping up and down celebrating the first eagle sighting on my land, I wrote "Breathtaking Closeness" to capture the moment. Then I returned my appreciation for his call by putting the poem on a picture of an eagle and hand-delivering it to him.

Appreciation is the key that unlocks the treasure chest of living in your Power and fulfilling your purpose. By choosing to *Journey in Appreciation*, you train your mind to remember your Innate Goodness, see the Innate Goodness in others and find the blessings in trying times as well as special ones, while appreciating those moments when you don't feel grateful at all. It shows you how to self-reflect, self-correct and self-motivate at crossroads moments. Like a plane on auto pilot, frequent expressions of appreciation keep you on course as you *Design and Live the Life* You *Love*.

"Appreciation is the key that unlocks the treasure chest of living in your Power and fulfilling your purpose."

What might come of genuinely appreciating yourself on days when you may not be eating well, following a restless night's sleep or when you are not getting enough exercise or nature time? Would your apology come across authentically after being abrupt with someone? Would it be easier to redirect your attention, so you satisfy your needs and bring the best of you to your activities?

What might you appreciate about people who fall into the *Projection Dilemma* in their interactions with you so you don't take their attitudes or behaviors personally? Would you be more inclined to be understanding and patient? Instead of forcing a solution or blaming people or events for your frustration, might you say, "Thank you for asking so many questions so I can practice patience and learn how to understand your point of view"? Well, maybe not directly to his or her face. But in your heart, might you appreciate how they perhaps invite you to communicate clearer boundaries, respectfully hold them accountable, ask directly for what you want or listen so they feel heard?

What would happen if you appreciated your sad, angry and fearful feelings and yourself for having them? Would you be kinder to yourself and others? When you hold back any feelings, you also limit your capacity to think clearly as well as to give and receive love. Your capacity to appreciate the complexities of life and find the niche that fulfills your Me, Inc. mission and purpose is governed by your comfort with all of your emotions. What miracle might come of honoring the rich texture of all of you and others? Would you be fulfilling your purpose?

Occasionally, you may hear an oppositional inner voice or feel resistance when you think or say how much you appreciate the family, friends and co-workers who push your buttons or when you think about the crossroads moments that stimulate your doubts or fears. Can you be truly grateful for this incongruence and the opportunity to practice the activities, tips and tools in this guide?

Being thankful as you ride the ups and downs along your path does not suggest that you

"Being thankful as you ride the ups and downs along your path does not suggest that you condone disrespectful or abusive behavior."

condone disrespectful or abusive behavior. You are not appreciating the hurtful behavior; you are giving thanks for the opportunity to practice being healthy when you ask for respectful exchanges. The following story is an example of how I dealt with my own reaction and journeyed the path of appreciation after allowing my buttons to be pushed.

One day, my youngest sister called and needed to vent. I listened without interruption. When she was finished, I asked whether she wanted feedback or to just have me listen. She opted for feedback then raged erratically when she didn't like what I said. I was angry that the rant came without warning and afraid to approach her about the incident. I felt attacked and chose to use the crossroads moment to overcome my freeze pattern so I could ask for nonviolent communication from her. To prepare my response, I wrote her a three-page letter attacking her back—which I did not mail. Instead, I didn't speak to her for several weeks. During that time, I used *The Resolution Steps* while rewriting the letter many times, until I could write the facts without fear or anger.

Three pages became one short paragraph: "It is not okay for you to rage at me. I listened and gave you feedback, as you requested. I do not deserve to be treated that way and would like an apology." Within a day of getting the letter, she called and apologized. I told her how much I appreciated her need to vent and how grateful I was that she trusted me with her feelings. Then I reminded her how our father raged, explaining that I no longer allow others to make me a target of their anger.

It was not in my best interest to let my fear of triggering another emotional outburst lead me to ignore my sister's Projection, Inc. CEO behavior. It was not in her best interest to continue to recycle her anger with me. By using this and other similar incidents to address my issue, I created an opening for her to stop perpetuating her negative reaction and for me to stop perpetuating strategies that allowed others to be unhealthy in relationship to me. I used the incident to put into action my Me, Inc. CEO mission, purpose and values and gave her permission to do the same by modeling the healthy self-expression I wanted from her.

How would your life be different if you appreciated that everyone and every crossroads moment is helping you become the Best Person you can be? If you looked with wonder in the mirror of every circumstance in your life, how might you engage the demanding, passion-driven boss, the co-worker who talks too much, the days when an extra expense hits unexpectedly or when there doesn't seem to be enough of you to go around at home?

"How would your life be different if you appreciated that everyone and every crossroads moment is helping you become the Best Person you can be?"

Does this mean you should be able to live without getting your buttons pushed? I don't know if you can ever be completely buttonless. I do know you can significantly reduce the number of buttons and their sensitivity by developing and living your *Me, Inc. Treasure Map*. Living it means practicing the skills in *Your Communication Toolkit*, walking *The Path of Courage*, practicing *A Nightly Forgiveness/Appreciation Moment* and periodically doing *The Resolution Steps*, while incorporating any additional resources you need to address your emotional triggers. If you were to do this, what do you think would happen? Would you be happier? Would you live in your Power, navigating the ups and downs of life's crossroads moments? What is the value in finding out?

Why Engage Crossroads Moments with Appreciation?

Engaging crossroads moments with a positive attitude is a choice and a skill. Appreciation is a daily practice for mastering this skill. People who look for blessings when reflecting on their day as well

"Engaging crossroads moments with a positive attitude is a choice and a skill. Appreciation is a daily practice for mastering this skill."

as those who meditate or commit random acts of kindness are more optimistic than those who do not. They are more able to flow with crossroads moments, allowing them to deepen relationships, solve problems and reveal new directions.

When you practice being thankful, you produce the happiness neurotransmitter, dopamine. If you are having difficulty thinking yourself into a better attitude, meditate or do something physical. When you walk, run, garden or dance, you activate more of your brain and stimulate the chemicals that support an optimistic outlook. Prove to yourself how your thoughts affect your physical energy and feelings by doing the following simple activity.

Prove it to Yourself

1. Start in a sitting position. First, think about a person you are upset with or a situation you are concerned about and feel the feelings that go with it. While thinking the thought and feeling the feelings, stand up. Notice how light or heavy you feel as you move.

2. Return to sitting. Then think of something or someone who you appreciate and smile. Again, stand up.

3. Notice the difference in effort used for each activity.

4. If moving from sitting to standing doesn't give you enough feedback, walk up a flight of stairs in place of the sitting-to-standing activity.

Figure 26.

Practice appreciating each new self-awareness. Express what you appreciate about someone before asking them to change a behavior. Review your *Me, Inc. Treasure Map* looking for a voice of appreciation in what you write. As you take action steps that challenge you to live in your Power, appreciate yourself for stepping up to the challenge. Be authentic as you do and you will enjoy growing levels of peace, happiness and synchronicity.

Clue #33: Expressing Appreciation of Others Can Sometimes Backfire

In school and in the business world, expressing appreciation for the work of others has been taught as a way to motivate people. Unfortunately, this approach has the potential of sabotaging a person's Innate Desire to learn and do his or her best. People can develop the habit of acting to please others, which is typically followed by the need to measure their worth by how others respond to their efforts. Remember what you learned about world mirrors in Clue #28, page 154. A desire to please can also be perceived as manipulative when it is motivated by the need to have someone respond in a particular way. How are you helping your children, peers or employees build their self-esteem when you appreciate them?

Giving appreciation can be sensitive. You may intend to be sincere and yet, if you regularly and hurriedly say, "I appreciate it" or "Thanks a lot" with a flat tone of voice while not looking someone in the eye, over time they might don a movie projector on their head and see you as someone who doesn't really care.

I am not advocating throwing out the practice of expressing appreciation of others. I am encouraging a more conscious approach, one that develops the Me, Inc. CEO in others. There is a way of giving appreciation that empowers others to be self-motivated, self-reflecting and self-correcting—to resource their Authentic Desire to do quality work not just to please a parent, boss or friend, but to please themselves because they love giving their best.

For example, instead of saying, "I am so proud of you...", we draw out the Innate Power of children when we get excited about what they have accomplished and say, "You must be so proud of yourself for making a new friend..." Instead of chiming, "You did a great job!" we draw out the Innate Power of others by saying, "You seem thrilled to have finished that project on time." The former can leave people unaware of what they did that was so great, in your opinion. In the latter approach, self-esteem is enhanced by teaching people to acknowledge their own efforts because you noticed specifically what they did well and how they felt about it. (A quick review of how to assertively communicate *Facts Versus Opinions* on page 145 will help you with this.)

By way of other examples, a scheduler can be the brunt of regular resistance because he or she cannot please everyone. An authentic "Thank you for all your efforts to accommodate everyone's needs, especially mine" will make their day as they look for ways to meet your request. Working mothers can feel overwhelmed by attempting to meet the many needs of people at work and at home. A truly grateful acknowledgment of their efforts at home and an offer to fix dinner and clean up afterwards models for children a loving partnership and feeds the cycle of appreciation.

"The ability to source Authentic Appreciation is mined on the quest for living in your Power."

The ability to source Authentic Appreciation is mined on the quest for living in your Power. If your expression of appreciation receives a negative response remember, the person is a mirror reflecting feedback about your motivation, timing and approach. When you live in your Power, you are self-motivated, self-reflecting and self-correcting. Clue #34 encourages you to use these moments for self-assessment and guides you through the process, so you learn whether you were a Me, Inc. CEO or Projection, Inc. CEO when a negative response occurs.

Clue #34: Crossroads Moments are Times for Self-Reflection

One day as I stood outside looking up at a sunny, late winter sky, my attention was diverted by the clear, strong shrill of a finch singing from atop the highest branch of a bare oak tree. The bird was not much bigger than the growing buds gathering energy to bloom in spring. Yet its song filled the valley. I watched and listened, amazed that such a little creature could sing so loudly, while thinking *How beautiful to have unobstructed self-expression!* Like the little songbird, we each have our own note to share and will share it as we appreciate ourselves and others and do what brings us joy.

The synchronicity of the arrival of this little bird, at the moment I took a break for some fresh air and reflection, was a mirror inviting me to contemplate how far I had come in my ability to communicate with individuals, groups and on paper. Abrupt encounters also invite self-reflection. Setting aside self-reflection time at difficult crossroads moments allows appreciation to replace judgment so you can perceive clearly and respond consciously. The following two self-reflection activities will help facilitate your self-reflection moments.

"How beautiful to have unobstructed self-expression!"

Self-Reflection Activity #1:
Return to Me, Inc.

Self-Reflection Activity #1 deepens your awareness of when you resign your position as Me, Inc. CEO in favor of being a Projection, Inc. CEO so you can think through strategies for minimizing your time there and return to Me, Inc. (Hint – just doing the exercise returns you to your position as CEO of Me, Inc.) Review the Figure 13 *Projection, Inc. CEO and Me, Inc. CEO Strategies* (page 121), then ask yourself the following questions:

1. How do I know when I am CEO of Projection, Inc.?

2. How do I view myself when I am CEO of Projection, Inc?

3. How do I view the other person or event?

4. How does my view affect their response to me or my reaction to the event?

5. Is my view of them or the situation true?

6. What is my win/win intention for this situation?

7. What "I" statement would best communicate this intention?

8. When is the best time to address this? (Hint: when emotions are calm.)

9. Is it safe to handle this alone? Do I feel safe? Do I need outside support?

10. What will happen if I don't address this? How will I feel? How important is it?

Self-Reflection Activity #2:
"Did I Cause it?"

Sometimes when you are communicating as a Me, Inc. CEO, people will still respond negatively. *Self-Reflection Activity #2* helps you evaluate whether you were at the helm of Me, Inc. or Projection, Inc. when someone negatively mirrors your approach.

1. Was I abrupt, impatient or frustrated when communicating?

2. Was I trying to be nice or please them so I could get them to do and say what I wanted?

3. Was I attached to my agenda and dominating the conversation?

4. Was I trying to change them as a person?

5. Was I resisting their behavior or the situation?

6. Was I inflating their faults?

7. Was I inflating my own virtues?

8. Was I making any assumptions I would do well to confirm? What assumption was I making?

9. Was I genuinely caring about them as a person?

10. Was I open to seeing them or the situation differently?

If you answer, *No* to 1 through 8 and *Yes* to 9 and 10, you were being a Me, Inc. CEO.

Figure 27.

Clue #35: The Practice of Appreciation is a Magnet

When you reflect on and write about the ups and downs of your life looking for the value, significance and magnitude of their contributions to your personal or professional growth, you become a magnet attracting more of what you appreciate.

As an example, a client called for assistance with recovering from adverse personal and business events. While blaming others for how her life wasn't working, she sought confidence so she could pick herself up and move on. In session, self-reflection and other activities enabled her to return to her Me, Inc. CEO role. With greater confidence in her abilities, she was inspired to take responsibility for what she could do to enhance her self-esteem and rebound from her setbacks. Within the week, she called to express her appreciation for the work we had done and the gratitude she felt. She shared that she had attracted two new clients and had taken action to resolve her relationship issue. Going forward, her practice is to appreciate what she sees in her world mirror and make adjustments when noticing negative reflections, so her attraction magnet stays strong. Here are some suggestions I gave her as well as some activities I have recommended to others I coach.

"When you reflect on and write about the ups and downs of your life looking for the value, significance and magnitude of their contributions to your personal or professional growth, you become a magnet attracting more of what you appreciate."

Activities for Practicing Appreciation

1. Keep an appreciation journal.
   Reflect daily on anyone and anything you appreciate and write at least five of them down. When you have tough times, it is great to go back to your journal and remember that, even in tough times, there is much to appreciate.

2. Make appreciation moments part of your mealtime conversations.
   At dinner with your family or friends, have an end-of-the-day-go-around in which everyone shares something they appreciate about their day. If someone focuses on problems, empathize by saying something like, "Sounds like you had a tough day." When they are done complaining and feel heard ask, "And what are you thankful for?"

3. Do what brings you joy.
   The things you love to do are the building blocks of an optimistic outlook and a happy life. Do you love to visit with friends, go to movies, dance, draw, write, sing, hike, ride horses or just have private moments, in silence? At the office, do you love getting organized, tackling innovative projects or connecting with associates before jumping into the day? When you regularly do the things you enjoy, you bring that happiness to all areas of your life.

4. Take charge of your state of mind by taking good care of yourself. You are less likely to resign your position as Me, Inc. CEO when you are rested and nourished.
   a. Get a good night's sleep. Eight hours is optimal.
   b. Sip water throughout the day.
   c. Eat healthy food and snacks.

(continued next page)

d. Take breaks every hour or so.

e. Smile often at others and when you look at yourself in the mirror.

f. At the end of the day, review and resolve any events in which you became Projection, Inc. CEO by enjoying *A Nightly Forgiveness/Appreciation Moment.*

5. Cultivate a sense of humor.

Marvel at how similar your boss is to the parent, relative or teacher who insisted that everything be spit-shined to a high gloss and put away in the same place after each use. Noticing similarities between the personalities of people presently in your life and people in your past can make you chuckle with amazement at how they can be so alike. When you bring wonder to your perception of others, you also seed appreciation of people and their unique ways of being.

6. Express appreciation as you go about your day.

A friend of mine has a new-found appreciation for going to the store after being housebound following a surgery. Although it is not fun, time without motivates you to be thankful for the little things in life. Why not be mindful of what you are doing and be thankful now?

a. Celebrate the sun while walking on a bright-blue-sky day.

b. Brush your teeth while feeling grateful to have them.

c. Use your household appliances, appreciating their ease and convenience.

d. Love the dishes, faces, hands and feet you wash.

e. Appreciate the money you do have.

Figure 28.

Clue #36: Completions are Crossroads Moments

One or more crossroads moments led you to pick up this guide seeking answers and solutions. Rather than attempting to give those to you, I started by asking you to consider that your crossroads moments are inviting you to reflect on where you are and where you have been, before figuring out where you are going. I asked you to embrace them for discovering and reconnecting with your Innate Power, the best source for all your answers. I introduced you to the *Projection Dilemma* and recommended activities that allow you to make choices from clear perception. I have also shown you how to *Design and Live the Life* You *Love* from your Power, so you can create happy and meaningful outcomes whether you go in new directions or become more comfortable where you are. Guidepost by guidepost, I have taken you on a journey that enables you to live in your Power and fulfill your purpose.

As you walk your path, you will experience many interim and final completions. The future, no matter how well visioned and mapped, is unknown. As you quest, appreciate each of your achievements and setbacks. When the moment passes and you stand on the threshold of *What's next?*, revisit your *Me, Inc. Treasure Map* and affirm your intention before proceeding. When you embrace interim advances or regressions and the variety of inner responses they bring, you make space for fresh eyes and motivation to choose your next direction.

When you embrace interim advances or regressions and the variety of inner responses they bring, you make space for fresh eyes and motivation to choose your next direction.

Celebrate and allow a settling into the experience of an ending before beginning again. Let yourself decompress from all the effort you exerted to get where you are. Feel your joy and satisfaction. Feel your sadness and fear. Yes, sadness and fear can arise because you are letting go of the process of creating something important to you. Remember, it is your perception rather than the event itself that fuels your feelings. Before focusing on your next steps, reflect on where you began and how you are now different. Are you a kinder, wiser and more skilled person? More sustainable than enjoying your passing achievements, be with the happiness that arises from crossing the threshold to what's next while being aware of your inner shifts. Allow yourself to feel the wisdom that all things pass. What always remains is Essential You.

"Allow yourself to feel the wisdom that all things pass. What always remains is Essential You."

Some of us can be challenged to find completion points in projects and relationships. Each moment of resting with what is done seems to bring new ideas and hopes as well as resistance. Where there is resistance, we can find many reasons for not being done. For those of us who struggle with bringing closure, we stand at a crossroads moment. One possibility is to let indecision and fear keep us from our treasure. Another is to embrace the clues and do the activities that reveal the courage, clarity and joy of stepping into what's next from our Power.

I lived the writing of this guidebook as a treasure hunt, rewriting and editing it a number of times over many years. Not infrequently, I used *A Nightly Forgiveness/Appreciation Moment, The Resolution Steps* and the *Activities for Practicing Appreciation* with the intention of upgrading my *Projection Dilemma* voices so I could write from my Greater Self. As I bring this guide to a close, I celebrate the help I received and the Self I birthed as a result of living its principles each step of the way.

Completions mark new beginnings. Whatever your desires and crossroads moments, smile a knowing inner smile and embrace them for mining your Inner Treasure. May you journey, feeling Its breathtaking closeness.

T h e   G a p

Be with
t h e   g a p
between endings
and beginnings.

Relish
a no-time remembrance
before lumbering into
more doing.

Enter your cave
hibernate with the bear inside you
allow stores of fat and thick fur
to gestate yearnings.

Let your next cycle
be more
than habitual wanderings
grabbing more berries and meat.

Harness the natural rhythm
that awakens deep dreamers
and births new ways of being
come spring.

"There is no doubt that you must seek your treasure
But as you search, remember—
Ideas and opinions are cultivated things,
And treasures are not found in cultivated spots.
Wherever and whatever it is, your treasure
Lies buried in bewilderment."

(Mathnawi I, 2447)

—Rumi,
A Gift of Love: A Calendar of Rumi's Poetry for 2004

Additional Reading and Resources

Barks, Coleman. *The Essential Rumi: New Expanded Edition.* New York: Harper Collins, 2004.

Blake, William. *The Complete Poetry and Prose of William Blake: New Revised Edition.* New York: Anchor Books, 1988.

Blum, Ralph. *The Book of Runes.* New York: St. Martins Press, 1982.

Brainy Quotes. *Morehei Ueshiba Quotes.* *www.brainyquotes.com.* Website. Brainy Quote Desktop. 2001.

Brennan, Barbara Ann. *Hands of Light: A Guide to Healing Through the Human Energy Field.* New York: Bantam Books, 1987.

Canfield, Jack and Mark Victor Hansen. *A 3rd Serving of Chicken Soup for the Soul: 101 More Stories to Open the Heart and Rekindle The Spirit.* Deerfield Beach: Health Communications, Inc., 1996.

Canfield, Jack and Jacqueline Miller. *Heart at Work.* New York, San Francisco, Washington D.C.: McGraw Hill, 1996.

Covey, Steven R. *The Seven Habits of Highly Effective People: Powerful Lessons in Personal Change.* New York: Simon and Schuster, 1989, 2004.

Dennison, Paul E, Ph.D. and Gail E. Dennison. *Brain Gym Teacher's Edition: The Companion Guide to Brain Gym: Simple Activities for Whole-Brain Learning.* Ventura: Hearts At Play, Inc., 2010.

Dyer, Dr. Wayne. *The Power of Intention: Learning to Co-create Your World Your Way.* Hay House, Inc. *www.hayhouse.com,* 2010.

Gratitude 365. APP. *www.gratitude365app.com*

Harris, Dan. *10% Happier: How I Tamed The Voice In My Head, Reduced Stress Without Losing My Edge, And Found Self-Help That Actually Works—A True Story.* New York: HarperCollins Publishers, 2014.

Jones, Laurie Beth. *The Path: Creating Your Mission Statement for Work and for Life.* New York: Hyperion, 1996.

Leonard, George. *Mastery: The Keys to Success and Long-term Fulfillment.* New York: Plume, 1992.

Lipton, Bruce, Ph.D. *The Biology of Belief: Unleashing the Power of Consciousness, Matter, and Miracles.* Santa Rosa: Mountain of Love/Elite Books, 2005.

Kaufman, Barry Neil. *Happiness is a Choice.* New York: Random House, 1991.

Markova, Dawna, Ph.D. *The Open Mind: Exploring the 6 Patterns of Natural Intelligence: Unlocking the Pattern of Your Natural Intelligence for Insight, Creativity & Better Communication.* York Beach: Conari Press, 1996.

O'Dea, James. *Cultivating Peace: Becoming a 21st—Century Peace Ambassador.* San Rafael: Shift Books, 2012.

Oliver, Mary. *Thirst.* Boston: Beacon Press, 2006.

Oliver, Mary. *New & Selected Poems: Volume One.* Boston: Beacon Press, 1992.

Pearce, Joseph Chilton. *The Biology of Transcendence: A Blueprint of the Human Spirit.* Rochester: Park Street Press, 2002.

Perdue, Deborah. *Grace of Gratitude Journal.* www.graceofgratitude.com

Pert, Candace B., Ph.D. *Molecules of Emotion: The Science Behind Mind-Body Medicine.* New York: Touchstone, 1997.

Pink, Dan H. *Drive: The Surprising Truth About What Motivates Us.* New York: Riverhead Books, 2009.

Rosenberg, Marshall. *Nonviolent Communication: A Language of Life.* Encinitas: Puddle Dancer Press, 2003.

Stafford, William. *Ask Me: 100 Essential Poems.* Minneapolis: Graywolf Press, 2014.

Stone, Hal and Sidra. *Embracing Your Inner Critic: Turning Self-Criticism into a Creative Asset.* Albion: HarperOne, 1993.

Tolle, Eckhart. *The Power of Now: A Guide to Spiritual Enlightenment.* Novato: New World Library, 1999.

Whyte, David. *Crossing the Unknown Sea: Work as a Pilgrimage of Identity.* New York: Riverhead Books, 2001.

Whyte, David. *Heart Aroused: Poetry and the Preservation of the Soul in Corporate America.* New York: Currency/Doubleday, 2002.